THE MARKETING PLANNING COACH

Eric Davies

The Teach Yourself series has been trusted around the world for over 60 years. It has helped millions of people to improve their skills and achieve their goals. This new 'Coach' series of business books is created especially for people who want to focus proactively on a specific workplace skill and to get a clear result at the end of it. Whereas many business books help you talk the talk, the Coach will help you walk the walk.

THE MARKETING PLANNING COACH

Eric Davies

First published in Great Britain in 2014 by Hodder & Stoughton. An Hachette UK company.

First published in US in 2014 by The McGraw-Hill Companies, Inc.

Copyright © Eric Davies 2014

The right of Eric Davies to be identified as the Author of the Work has been asserted by him in accordance with the Copyright, Designs and Patents Act 1988.

Database right Hodder & Stoughton (makers)

The Teach Yourself name is a registered trademark of Hachette UK.

British Library Cataloguing in Publication Data: a catalogue record for this title is available from the British Library.

Paperback ISBN 978 1 471 80157 0

Library of Congress Catalog Card Number: on file.

10 9 8 7 6 5 4 3 2 1

The publisher has used its best endeavours to ensure that any website addresses referred to in this book are correct and active at the time of going to press. However, the publisher and the author have no responsibility for the websites and can make no guarantee that a site will remain live or that the content will remain relevant, decent or appropriate.

The publisher has made every effort to mark as such all words which it believes to be trademarks. The publisher should also like to make it clear that the presence of a word in the book, whether marked or unmarked, in no way affects its legal status as a trademark.

Every reasonable effort has been made by the publisher to trace the copyright holders of material in this book. Any errors or omissions should be notified in writing to the publisher, who will endeavour to rectify the situation for any reprints and future editions.

Typeset by Cenveo® Publisher Services.

Printed and bound in Great Britain by CPI Group (UK) Ltd, Croydon CR0 4YY.

Hodder & Stoughton policy is to use papers that are natural, renewable and recyclable products and made from wood grown in sustainable forests. The logging and manufacturing processes are expected to conform to the environmental regulations of the country of origin.

Hodder & Stoughton Ltd

338 Euston Road

London NW1 3BH

www.hodder.co.uk

CONTENTS

MEET THE COACH

Eric Davies is a professional marketing expert who has led many marketing courses for a range of institutions including the Chartered Institute of Management. He also runs his own consultancy working with a wide range of clients; past clients include BT, Capita and the RAC. His own postgraduate research focused on the relationship between marketing strategy and company performance.

Eric Davies is also the author of *Successful Marketing in a Week* (Teach Yourself, 2012). In addition, he has contributed articles to a number of journals including *Accountancy, European Journal of Marketing, The Pakistan Management Review, Management Consultancy* and *The Municipal Journal*.

HOW TO USE THIS BOOK

 OUTCOMES FROM THIS CHAPTER

- Learn who will benefit from this workbook.
- Discover what you will get out of completing the workbook.
- Find out what marketing planning is and who should be involved in the marketing planning process.

The purpose of this workbook is to take you, step by step, through the process of marketing planning so that you will be able to produce your own effective marketing plan – one that can be implemented and monitored and that will help you achieve your objectives. As the writer, my job is to 'coach' you in this process – to guide and support you in developing your marketing plan.

Before we start, let's take some time to consider the terminology associated with marketing. Like most relatively modern disciplines, the language of marketing is populated by many words in common usage, such as 'customer', 'segment' and 'positioning'. To avoid ambiguity, we will define these terms as they relate to marketing when they are introduced in the text. Throughout the text you will see references to 'organization', which in this context refers equally to profit-focused businesses large and small, self-employed individuals and start-up businesses, as well as not-for-profit institutions such as the public sector and charities. In addition, the term 'product' describes any tangible or intangible offering that delivers benefits to customers.

WHO IS THIS WORKBOOK FOR?

Marketing is now a key discipline in organizing and directing not only large consumer-focused businesses but also a wide range of organizations including service-based businesses, business-to-business organizations and small and medium-sized enterprises (SMEs). In fact, developing a marketing plan is as important for a start-up business as it is for a multinational. In addition, not-for-profit organizations (such as the public sector, charities and social enterprises) are also seeing the benefits of using the disciplines and tools of marketing to help them achieve their objectives.

This workbook is therefore designed to meet the needs of a wide range of readers, including:

- start-up business owners
- owners and managers of SMEs
- senior and middle managers in larger businesses with responsibility for marketing (i.e. whether at a business level or within a profit centre) both in for-profit and not-for-profit organizations
- non-marketing middle managers in larger businesses taking on a marketing role or wishing to better understand the processes involved in marketing planning
- junior managers seeking to enhance their knowledge and skills.

HOW SHOULD YOU USE THE WORKBOOK?

The workbook is designed to guide you through each stage in the marketing planning process. Each chapter focuses on a stage in the process. To get the most benefit from the workbook, read and work through each chapter in turn. It may be worth reading through the whole book to get an overview of its contents before you start your own planning process in detail.

The book is a mixture of interactive exercises ('coaching sessions') and commentary text. Each chapter describes a different stage of the marketing planning process and includes a series of coaching sessions related to that stage, designed to improve your understanding and guide you towards the production of your marketing plan. In addition, there are online tools available, in support of Chapters 4, 6 and 8, which can be downloaded from:

www.TYCoachbooks.com/Marketingplanning

The exercises are not just there to make you think. The idea is to involve you in the process of acquiring a better understanding of the subject matter through practical experience. It is best to complete the exercises in the order they appear, because later text will often provide commentary on their outcomes.

Each chapter has the following features:

OUTCOMES FROM THIS CHAPTER

A bullet list at the start of each chapter sets out exactly what you will have got from that chapter by the time you have finished it. This is in terms of both what you will have *learned* (e.g. from the running text) and what you will have *done* (e.g. in the 'coaching sessions').

COACHING SESSIONS

These are the key, meaty features within each chapter that will get you really working on, and interacting with, the ideas given in the commentary text. They include self-assessments, checklists and reflective questions.

COACH'S TIPS

These are key, 'snappy' pieces of advice, often drawn from the author's own experience.

NEXT STEPS

This is an end-of-chapter section summarizing what you have learned and placing that learning in the context of the chapters that follow.

TAKEAWAYS

Three or four reflective questions at the end of each chapter will help you focus on how what you have read and done in that chapter has helped you, *personally*.

What counts at the end of the day, after all, is what *you* get out of the book, what you take away with you when you've finished reading it, and how much of what you've learned is information you can use.

WHAT IS MARKETING PLANNING?

Marketing planning seeks to apply a logical and objective approach to deciding how an organization's capabilities will be matched to opportunities in the marketplace, so that the objectives of the organization can be met.

We first need to understand what marketing is. In essence, marketing is a business philosophy that says it is *easier* to achieve your business objectives if you *understand* and *meet* customers' *needs*. Customers should be the *raison d'être* of the business.

There are three main approaches to organizing a business:

- **Production orientation**

This approach developed at the time of the Industrial Revolution in the UK (roughly 1750–1850), when goods were generally scarce. Producers could sell all they could produce and therefore the focus was on production and distribution at the lowest cost.

- **Sales orientation**

From the late nineteenth and early twentieth centuries, competition grew and the focus turned to selling goods by persuading buyers to choose the seller's product, regardless of whether it was the best match to their needs. A clear problem with this approach was that, if the product did not meet the customer's needs, they would not purchase it again, which meant no repeat sales, which would affect the survival of the business.

- **Customer or marketing orientation**

Marketing theories really developed from the 1950s onwards, when most markets displayed intense competition for customers. For a business to succeed it had to gain customers from its competitors, and this competition drove a need to understand and satisfy customers' requirements. In essence, this approach put the customer at the centre of a firm's thinking and strategy.

COACHING SESSION 1

What's the business orientation?

Consider the following business sectors. In your opinion, are they predominantly production, sales or marketing oriented?

Business sector	Production oriented	Sales oriented	Marketing oriented
Automobiles			
Banking & finance			
Energy supply (gas & electricity)			
Computing & software			

How would you describe your own organization's orientation?

_____

The four 'big ideas' in marketing

There are four 'big ideas' in marketing that are worth setting out:

1. **Exchange** – at the heart of marketing is the process of enabling individuals and organizations to obtain what they need and want through exchanges with others.

2. **Promise** – in establishing and maintaining customer relationships, the seller gives a set of **promises** based on the performance of a product or service offered – i.e. the benefits inherent in the offering that the seller believes are matched to the needs of the customer. In return, the buyer promises to meet his/her commitment in the exchange, generally some form of payment.

3. **Matching** – marketing is a matching process – matching the *benefits* in the organization's offerings with the *needs* of customers.

4. **'Customer' or 'marketing' orientation** – a business or organization that is customer (or marketing) oriented puts the needs of the customer at the centre of its thinking and strategy.

COACHING SESSION 2

Ranking the important factors

Rank the following factors in terms of your view of how important they are in determining whether or not a business is marketing oriented.

Factor	Very important	Important	Not important	Not at all important
Being the cheapest				
Understanding customers' perceived needs				
Having the highest-quality product				
Having the largest advertising budget				
Having a world-famous celebrity endorse one's product				
Having an ongoing investment in marketing research				
Having an ongoing focus on competitors and the general business environment				

When you have completed the list, you may want to look at the commentary in Appendix 1.

Many individuals within organizations are involved in making decisions and taking actions in a wide range of marketing-related areas – for example, deciding what to offer to the market, setting prices, selecting where products or services should be made available to customers, designing advertisements and sales messages and investing in promotional activities to inform and persuade customers, and making sales.

Marketing planning seeks to co-ordinate the wide range of marketing activities to ensure the most effective use of resources and the best match of the organization's capabilities to customer needs. Research, some of which we shall consider later, suggests that this approach is associated with improved organizational performance.

COACHING SESSION 3

What do you already know about marketing?

Below are some aspects of marketing. Indicate your level of knowledge of each one by circling the appropriate number from 1 to 7, where 1 is little or no knowledge and 7 is a full working knowledge of the subject.

The marketing orientation	1	2	3	4	5	6	7
Market segmentation	1	2	3	4	5	6	7
Buyer behaviour	1	2	3	4	5	6	7
Marketing research	1	2	3	4	5	6	7
Product strategy	1	2	3	4	5	6	7
Pricing strategy	1	2	3	4	5	6	7
Distribution strategy	1	2	3	4	5	6	7
Promotional strategy	1	2	3	4	5	6	7

The following chapters deal with many of the areas listed above, but this exercise will help you identify those areas where you may wish to increase your knowledge through further reading. (A good place to start would be with *Successful Marketing In A Week* by the author of this workbook.)

Developing a marketing plan involves a series of four interrelated stages:

- **Analysis** – this stage focuses on analysing the current situation, both within the *organization* and in the *marketplace* (including customers, competitors and the broader business environment) in which it operates.

- **Planning** – this stage seeks to position the organization to maximize its strengths and exploit opportunities in the market environment, while minimizing the effects of the organization's weaknesses and the threats in the marketplace.

- **Implementation** – once the most effective strategy has been identified, it is critical to ensure that action is taken to deploy or implement the strategy to achieve its desired objectives.

- **Control** – this stage is concerned with ensuring that the plan achieves its defined objectives. This involves making sure that the defined stages are implemented correctly and at the right time and that the plan responds to changes in the market environment.

Marketing planning has been described as 'anticipatory decision making' – that is, making decisions now about what will happen in the future. Since change is constant in all facets of our lives and we can never completely predict the future, we might wonder why it is worth spending time on marketing planning when some unforeseen event can make all that work irrelevant. There are two main reasons:

1. The process of planning helps managers identify the factors that may influence the future success of the business and allows them to take appropriate action. Eliminating such factors can give a manager more time to deal with unforeseen events.

2. Developing a plan forces a manager to evaluate the potential associated with different courses of action. Consequently, when new opportunities emerge, the manager has something to compare these with.

Fundamentally, the point of marketing planning comes in the payback. Research, which we shall review later, demonstrates that businesses that adopt the marketing planning process outperform businesses that do not, in the same industries and over the same time frames.

COACHING SESSION 4

What do you already know about your organization?

Rate your level of satisfaction with your knowledge of the following aspects of your organization by circling the appropriate number from 1 to 4, where 1 is very satisfied and 4 is very dissatisfied.

Which products or services provide the majority of your sales?	1	2	3	4
Which customer groups (or segments) provide the majority of your sales?	1	2	3	4
Which products or services provide the majority of your profits?	1	2	3	4
Which customer groups (or segments) provide the majority of your profits?	1	2	3	4

Later in the workbook we will introduce a series of exercises to help you enhance your understanding of your organization.

COACHING SESSION 5

What do you already know about your marketplace?

Rate your level of satisfaction with your knowledge of the following aspects of your marketplace by circling the appropriate number from 1 to 4, where 1 is very satisfied and 4 is very dissatisfied.

Who your customers are	1	2	3	4
What your customers' perceived needs are	1	2	3	4
What your customers' perceptions of value (i.e. benefits at price) are	1	2	3	4
Who your competitors are	1	2	3	4
What their strengths and weaknesses are	1	2	3	4
What the political, economic, social and technological (PEST) factors are that impact on your marketplace	1	2	3	4

Later in the workbook we will introduce a series of exercises to help you enhance your understanding of your marketplace.

WHO SHOULD BE INVOLVED IN MARKETING PLANNING?

It is acceptable for one individual to execute the marketing planning process and draft the marketing plan. However, adopting a team approach – setting up a **marketing planning team** – adds two significant benefits:

- Additional individuals bring knowledge and experience that can aid the planning process.

- Engaging the people who will be involved in implementing the plan helps to overcome the problem of 'lack of ownership'. It is important that the people who have to implement the plan are given the opportunity to contribute to its development.

Quite often, people think that it is only the marketing department that can deal with marketing issues. It is true that, in large consumer-based businesses for instance, there is a need for a range of sophisticated marketing management input and, consequently, the marketing department does have a major input into the marketing plan. However, if we think of marketing as the way an organization *engages* with its marketplace, clearly the *entire* organization needs to be 'marketing oriented' – i.e. focused on meeting the needs of the customers. This can mean that the members of the marketing planning team can be drawn from a wide range of disciplines within the organization. The two key questions are whether they can add value to the planning process and whether they are going to be involved in its implementation.

Moreover, some organizations such as small and medium-sized enterprises (SMEs) do not have the resources to support a separate marketing department. In the case of a start-up, there may be only one or two people involved. In such situations, managers may involve individuals from outside their organization to participate in the planning process; for example professional advisers (such as accountants), colleagues, or friends with business experience.

 COACH'S TIP

Factors to consider

Deciding who should be involved in the marketing planning process is really a function of the nature of your organization and the resources available.

COACHING SESSION 6

Deciding who to include in your team

In the table below, write down the names and job titles of the people you think need to be a part of your marketing planning team, including your view of their level of involvement ('H' high, 'M' medium, 'L' low) in the planning and implementation stages.

Name	Job title	Planning	Implementation

WHAT WILL YOU GET OUT OF COMPLETING THE WORKBOOK?

This workbook has two key objectives:

- It will give you knowledge and understanding of the process of developing an effective marketing plan so that you will be able to produce one at any time in the future.

- It will enable you to produce a marketing plan that you can implement within your organization now, and monitor over time to measure its success.

⚇ COACHING SESSION 7

What do you want to get out of the workbook?

In the table below, write down your personal objectives in the left-hand column and in the right-hand column rank them in importance – writing 1 for most important.

Personal objective	Rank (in importance)

When you have completed the workbook, you should return to this table, to check that you have achieved your personal objectives.

1 WHAT IS MARKETING?

 OUTCOMES FROM THIS CHAPTER

- Define what marketing is.
- Understand why marketing is important in helping organizations achieve their objectives.
- Know what key activities are involved in marketing.
- See how marketing strategy relates to other aspects of the organization.

THE DEFINITION OF MARKETING

We have already learned that marketing is a business philosophy that says it is easier to achieve your business objectives if you understand and meet customers' needs. We also set out the four 'big ideas' in marketing:

1. **Exchange:** enabling individuals and organizations to obtain what they need and want through exchanges with others
2. **Promise:** selling a set of promises about a good or service for a promise from the buyer to commit to the exchange
3. **Matching:** matching benefits to needs
4. **'Customer' or 'marketing' orientation:** focusing on the needs of the customer.

In this chapter we are going to consider the nature and the value of marketing as a way of directing an organization and increasing the probability of successfully achieving the goals of the organization.

⧉⧉ COACHING SESSION 8

Your definition of marketing

From your experience and what you've read so far, what would be your definition of marketing?

Write your definition below:

_____

_____

_____

_____

_____

The Chartered Institute of Marketing (CIM) developed a commonly used definition of marketing:

> 'Marketing is the management process responsible for identifying, anticipating and satisfying customer requirements profitably.'

⧉⧉ COACHING SESSION 9

Compare your definition

Compare your definition with that of CIM. How does it compare? Do you agree with their definition? Can you see any weaknesses in their definition?

Write your thoughts below:

_____

_____

_____

_____

_____

The CIM's definition captures many elements of the four big ideas listed above. However, this definition was created in the late 1970s and much has changed since then. CIM acknowledged this by commissioning their Director of Research & Information to develop the following revised definition for the twenty-first century:

> '[Marketing is] the strategic business function that creates value by stimulating, facilitating and fulfilling customer demand. It does this by building brands, nurturing innovation, developing relationships, creating good customer service and communicating benefits. With a customer-centric view, marketing brings positive return on investment, satisfies shareholders and stakeholders from business and the community, and contributes to positive behavioural change and a sustainable business future.'

> (Source: *Shape the Agenda, Tomorrow's World, Re-evaluating the role of Marketing,* David Thorp, CIM, 2007)

While we can see the core themes of the 1970s definition above, this new definition is broader, emphasizing 'building brands, nurturing innovation, developing relationships and creating good customer service and communicating benefits'. In addition, the definition includes references to the wider stakeholder community and to sustainability.

WHY MARKETING IS IMPORTANT

We have said that it is easier to achieve your business objectives if you understand and meet customers' needs. In essence, this is the fundamental reason why marketing is important in helping organizations achieve their objectives.

All markets are subject to pressures that drive down profits over time. The main pressures are:

- competition from rival organizations
- threats from new entrants to the market
- threats from products or services that substitute for your offering
- the bargaining power of strong suppliers and strong customers.

To 'beat the market' you have to have advantages over your competitors that are valued by your customers and these advantages have to be robust and responsive in the face of onrushing market forces.

☺☺ COACHING SESSION 10

Evaluating a case study

Consider the following case study.

Case study: TNT

TNT is a global business and the market leader in business-to-business (B2B) express delivery services, delivering up to 150 million items per year. It has the largest individual share of the national market and employs over 10,000 people across the UK and Ireland.

In 2008 TNT recognized that the increasing expectations of customers meant that the business had to make major changes to ensure that it could meet their needs. In-depth research showed that customer satisfaction depended not just on the process of delivering the service, but also on how the service was carried out. This resulted in TNT adopting a core strategy focused on delivering a quality customer experience. It developed a two-year programme to implement and communicate its *Customer Promise* to employees and customers.

In order to achieve the levels of process innovation and continuous improvement that the customer focus strategy required, TNT also needed to ensure that the capabilities of its people were aligned to this, particularly in delivering a high-quality customer experience. A review of new employees to the company showed that only 10 per cent held qualifications above QCF (Qualifications and Credit Framework) level 2, compared to the industry norm of 52 per cent (as identified by Skills for Logistics Research).

TNT's *Customer Promise* reflects its core strategy of customer focus and aligns with its corporate values to influence the organization's culture.

(Source, and for the full case study, visit: http://businesscasestudies.co.uk/tnt/delivering-a-superior-customer-experience/introduction.html#ixzz2Tvto7lCp)

What do you think are the most important aspects of the TNT case study from a marketing standpoint?

1 _____

2 _____

3 _____

4 _____

5 _____

There are some interesting themes in this case study:

- TNT recognized that their customers' perceived needs were changing.
- They used market research to obtain a clear, objective picture of how these needs were changing.
- TNT responded to this evidence by changing their strategy to focus on delivering a quality customer experience.
- TNT created their *Customer Promise* to make a more tangible idea that both customers and TNT staff could understand and identify with.
- This change meant that the entire business had to adopt this focus and every aspect of the business had to be aligned with their new strategy, e.g. staff training.

THE KEY ACTIVITIES INVOLVED IN MARKETING

If we return to CIM's definition of marketing as 'the management process responsible for identifying, anticipating and satisfying customer requirements profitably', we can think about the key activities involved in marketing.

COACHING SESSION 11

Key marketing activities

What do you think are the activities that you think are likely to be involved in marketing? Write your list below.

_____

_____

_____

_____

_____

_____

_____

_____

_____

_____

Now compare your list with this one:

- Identifying customer needs
- Quantifying market size and trends
- Defining customer segmentation
- Quantifying customer segment size and trends
- Monitoring the activities of competitors
- Monitoring the market environment – political, economic, societal and technological – and assessing the effect on our marketplace (customers, competitors and ourselves)
- Defining how we are going to deliver benefits to the customers' perceived needs (the product strategy)
- Setting prices so that the benefits in the product are seen by customers as representing good value, while meeting the organization's need for profit (the pricing strategy)
- Selecting where products are to be made available to the customer (the place or distribution strategy)
- Creating promotional messages and designing promotional campaigns that inform and persuade customers of the benefits of the product matched to their needs (the promotional strategy)
- Developing procedures that make it easy for customers to buy the product (the sales process)
- Providing after-sales service to foster and support brand loyalty among customers.

This list is by no means exhaustive but it provides you with a comparison with your own list.

COACHING SESSION 12

Comparing lists of marketing activities

Compare the list you created in the previous coaching session with the list above. Are there any activities that are in your list that are not in the list above?

Write down those activities below:

_____

_____

_____

_____

_____

Are there any activities in the list above that are not in your list?

Write down those activities below:

_____

_____

_____

_____

_____

Let us consider some of the most important activities associated with marketing, to do with identifying customer needs.

Identifying customer needs

We first need to answer the question, 'Who are our customers?' At first sight this might seem a simple question, with the answer, 'Our customers are the people who buy our products or services.' However, customers can range from individuals and families to small and medium-sized businesses, public limited companies (plcs) and government departments.

There can also be a difference between those who buy our product and those who 'consume' it. Take the example of a parent buying a product for their child, or someone buying a present for a friend. In business-to-business markets, specifiers and buyers are not necessarily the people who use the product being purchased. So we need to understand the relationship between purchase and consumption.

Customer behaviour

Customers develop their perception of their needs based on an interaction between their motives, values and attitudes. Customer behaviour has traditionally been seen as a problem-solving process. Implicit in this is that customers act in a logical manner when selecting solutions to their needs. The steps in such a process are set out below:

Problem recognition

↓

Information search

↓

Evaluation of options

↓

Product choice

↓

Outcomes

It is at stage 1, problem recognition, that the customer articulates their perceived needs – in essence a hierarchical list of requirements that the ideal product must be able to satisfy. The customer then proceeds to stage 2 – a search for information about potential solutions to their perceived needs. This leads to stage 3 – an evaluation of options – comparing the benefits of different products against the customer's perceived needs, in effect looking for the best *match*. At this stage, the customer is also considering the *value* inherent in each option: value can be defined as total benefits divided by price. Ultimately, this process leads to a product choice and the post-purchase stage (outcomes) where the customer 'consumes' the product and makes a judgement about how well or poorly it has met his needs. Clearly, this has an impact on repeat purchases and ultimately on brand loyalty.

COACH'S TIP

Do your research

Organizations use marketing research to gather information about customers' perceptions of their needs. Effective research can reduce risk in decision-making in a wide range of marketing activities, from product design and pricing through to decisions concerning where the product should be sold (distribution channels) and how best to promote the product to potential customers (what messages are going to inform and persuade them and where to place advertisements so that they will be exposed to the messages).

Market segmentation

Customers are different from one another in many ways – for example, in their values and attitudes, their incomes, age, gender and location. These differences are the reason why marketing managers seek to *segment* markets. Segmentation refers to dividing customers into segments where customers within one segment have similar characteristics and as a segment are different from customers in other segments.

We can imagine a number of ways in which customers can be organized as market segments. For example, there are geographical differences (countries, regions within countries, etc.), demographics (based on age, gender, family size, income, occupation, education, race, religion, etc.) and behavioural variations (consumer knowledge, perceptions, attitudes, uses of and responses to a product or service).

Market segmentation is strongly linked to business success. Research suggests that 80 per cent of variance in revenue growth is explained by choices about *where* to compete (i.e. which market segments) and only 20 per cent by *how* to compete. (Source: www.mckinsey.com/client_service/strategy/latest_thinking/granularity_of_growth)

It is therefore critical that we select the right market segments to compete in, to obtain the maximum advantage from our strengths.

THE MARKETING MIX (THE FOUR Ps)

The range of marketing activities is often referred to as the 'marketing mix'. The key idea is that a range of activities is necessary for delivering benefits to customers and each organization is likely to have a different mix of these activities as the basis for their strategy. Traditionally, marketers have thought in terms of four key strategic activities – product, price, place and promotion – known as the 'four Ps'. We can look at each of these elements in turn.

Product

Our 'product' carries benefits that satisfy customers' needs. While it can be a tangible, physical entity, 'product' can also be something intangible such as a service, an experience or an idea. Product strategy is the method by which we *satisfy* customers' needs.

A 'product' can be either wholly tangible or wholly intangible, or it might have some element of both tangible and intangible benefits as part of its appeal. Two extreme examples are:

- motorcars

  The physical nature of the product has a high element of tangibility, but there are intangible benefits such as the brand and dealer service.

- perfumes

    The core offering is intangible in terms of the benefits customers derive from the purchase but the offering is 'delivered' as a tangible product. Interestingly, part of this tangibility includes the packaging.

Sometimes there is confusion between product *benefits* and product *features*. Features are the product's capabilities; benefits are the outcomes customers 'consume' by way of meeting their perceived needs. In essence, product features *carry* product benefits.

Branding helps buyers identify products that might benefit them and tells them something about product quality and consistency. In frequent purchase situations it can also help customers save time. From the marketer's perspective, brand management seeks to make the product or service relevant to the target segments.

 COACH'S TIP

Understand branding

Brands should be seen as more than the difference between the actual cost of a product and its selling price: brands represent the sum of all valuable qualities of a product to the customer.

Price

At its basic level, price is the amount a customer must pay to obtain the benefit/s from a product or service – i.e. the *exchange* we referred to above. A key issue in pricing products is the customers' perception of value. *Value* is the customer's perception of the match of benefits in an offering to their needs and is measured by the customer's willingness to pay for it. For instance, if a customer is evaluating three products with *exactly* the same benefits matched to his or her needs, the one with the lowest price is the best value. However, if each of the three products is perceived to have *different* bundles of benefits, this makes assessing the value in each product much more difficult for the customer.

As we have seen, benefits can be tangible and intangible and products can carry a bundle of benefits relevant to a range of customers' needs. Consequently, the more sophisticated and/or complicated the product and the more variability in price levels, the more difficult it is for customers to make a value judgement and choose between different products.

Three interrelated forces that influence pricing decisions are:

- the target audience's perception of value in our and the competition's offerings
- our cost structure
- the competition's price levels.

Place

In its simplest terms and probably original sense, place is where the 'exchange' (of product or service for the price) takes place – the market square, for instance. In the modern context, the 'place' part of the marketing mix focuses on how products and services are distributed to customers, and this part of the marketing mix is also known as **distribution**.

There are two broad types of channel available to the marketer:

- **Intermediaries**

  These are independent organizations that carry out a number of activities associated with adding value to the marketing process. There are two main groups: retailers and wholesalers.

- **Direct**

  These organizations often choose to trade directly with customers, not only to reduce costs but also because of the potential for building customer relations. Direct channels can be broadly divided into two groups: traditional channels (such as direct mail) and new media (websites, e-commerce, etc.).

Promotion

Promotion is really about marketing communications and is concerned with *informing* and *persuading* customers. Promotion is the most visible part of the marketing mix and can be seen alongside general entertainment on TV, on the radio and in the cinema and also, increasingly, on the Internet. Ideally, marketing communications should manage the customer relationship over time, from pre-purchase to the ongoing relationship with the brand.

There are seven key decision areas involved in developing a promotional strategy:

1. Defining the target audience
2. Setting promotional objectives
3. Creating the message/s
4. Selecting the media
5. Creating the promotional programme
6. Setting the budget
7. Evaluating the results.

COACHING SESSION 13

Looking at a company's marketing mix

Read the following case study.

Case study: Aldi

Since opening its first store in 1913, Aldi has established itself as one of the most reputable retailers in the global business market by providing great value and quality. Aldi's goal is simple: 'to provide our customers with the products they buy regularly and ensure that those products are of the highest possible quality at guaranteed low prices'. Aldi's products are sourced from hand-picked suppliers whose products are sold under Aldi's own-brand labels.

A key focus of Aldi's marketing strategy is on demonstrating that Aldi brands are of equal quality to well-known brands such as Heinz and Fairy Liquid. To do this, Aldi ran blind taste tests among a cross section of shoppers. These confirmed that the majority of consumers who liked the famous brands also liked Aldi's brands. These findings formed the basis to Aldi's 'Like Brands' marketing campaign. This provided Aldi with a platform to communicate its quality and value messages effectively. Aldi's marketing mix therefore focuses on:

- Product – Aldi offers high-quality 'Like Brands'.

- Price – Aldi offers lower prices than its competitors without compromising on quality.

- Place – Aldi outlets are expanding globally.

- Promotions – Aldi uses a combination of above-the-line and below-the-line promotions with a focus on its 'Like Brands' and 'Swap & Save' campaigns.

Aldi has a distinctive approach to retailing that has given it a competitive advantage in a crowded marketplace. Its unique balance of the marketing mix enables it to provide high-quality, own-branded products at the lowest possible price. Aldi's innovative 'Like Brands' and 'Swap & Save' marketing campaigns are improving brand perceptions. They are aiding the achievement of Aldi's marketing objectives. The campaigns have increased sales per store by more than 100 per cent over three years by creating more loyal customers. Its multi-channel promotional activity is engaging consumers and creating positive feedback.

(Source and for the full case study: http://businesscasestudies.co.uk/aldi/creating-value-through-the-marketing-mix/introduction.html#ixzz2TvwSqOdc)

What do you think are the most important aspects of Aldi's marketing mix?

1 _____

2 _____

3 _____

4 _____

5 _____

HOW MARKETING STRATEGY RELATES TO OTHER ASPECTS OF THE ORGANIZATION

Marketing can be said to be the interface between the organization and the 'environment' in which it exists. Many current marketing writers focus on the importance of seeing marketing as a organization-wide issue and a wide range of studies has distilled **five** key behaviours that characterize businesses that have effectively (and profitably) made the customer/marketing orientation the operational basis of their businesses. These key behaviours are:

■ **Market sensing**

This is the foundation of an effective customer/marketing orientation; we must have objective and relevant information regarding our customers' needs.

■ **Quality focus**

The business must seek to improve product/service quality to maintain a competitive differential.

■ **Internal 'marketing'**

Quite simply, all employees must know what they have to do to satisfy customers' needs, must be able to do it and must be motivated to do it.

■ **Adaptive response**

It is critical that businesses are flexible and able to adapt to changing market conditions and customer needs. This includes understanding how broader political, economic, social and technological factors impact on our customers and competitors.

■ **External relationships**

The success of the business depends on how we interact with the outside world, so constructing effective means of two-way communication with customers is paramount.

→ NEXT STEPS

In this chapter we have:

- explored the definition of marketing
- considered why marketing is so important for organizations
- looked at some of the key behaviours that characterize a marketing-oriented organization
- offered a sound foundation upon which to build your understanding of the marketing planning process.

In the next chapter we will consider the evidence that supports the benefits of marketing planning for organizations. In addition, we will focus on the practical nature of effective marketing planning. We will also look at the most common pitfalls of planning as identified by research and how best to avoid these pitfalls.

TAKEAWAYS

How would you define marketing?

_____

_____

_____

_____

_____

_____

_____

_____

What are your thoughts on the differences between the widely used traditional definition of marketing (from the CIM) and their more recent definition for the twenty-first century?

_____

_____

_____

_____

_____

_____

_____

_____

Why do you think focusing on customers' needs is so fundamental to achieving an organization's businesses objectives?

_____

_____

_____

_____

_____

_____

_____

_____

Have you identified the key activities associated with marketing in your own organization –
identifying customer needs, market segmentation and the marketing mix (the four Ps)? How
and where are they carried out?

_____

_____

_____

_____

_____

_____

Having considered some of the key behaviours that characterize a marketing-oriented
organization – market sensing, quality focus, internal 'marketing', adaptive response and
(good) external relationships – how closely does your organization match these? Where are
the gaps?

_____

_____

_____

_____

_____

_____

2 THE BENEFITS AND PITFALLS OF MARKETING PLANNING

 OUTCOMES FROM THIS CHAPTER

- Understand the definition of marketing planning.
- Know what the benefits are of marketing planning for organizations.
- Understand the practical side of effective marketing planning.
- Be aware of the most common pitfalls in marketing planning and how to avoid them.

THE DEFINITION OF MARKETING PLANNING

Planning is something that most of us get involved in. A holiday, for instance, may need some planning so that essential tasks – obtaining visas and booking flights and hotels and so on – are done in good time. Planning helps us identify some of the factors that will influence the success of a venture and, while we may not be able to plan for all eventualities, at least we are taking steps to avoid problems that can be foreseen.

Here is a dictionary definition of 'planning':

> 'arranging beforehand, preparing, forming a plan (an especially detailed method by which a thing is done)'

Marketing planning, then, is simply the process by which the various aspects of marketing (including the marketing mix) are drawn together to produce a coherent basis for future action.

However, marketing planning is easier to talk about than to do. As we have seen, the process of marketing can involve a large number of interrelated decisions. We must develop a plan that is based not only on our knowledge of our organization but also on our understanding of our customers and potential customers (how they will act), our competitors (their plans and how they will react to our activities) and the general marketplace (our understanding of what political, economic, societal and technological forces may affect our marketplace). Clearly, we are facing a complex planning situation. Consequently, the *process* of marketing planning is designed to break down this complex activity into its component parts so that they may be dealt with sequentially to build to a final whole – the marketing plan.

Over the years, academics and researchers have conducted a wide range of work in the area of both defining marketing planning (i.e. the behaviours we must see in an organization before we can say that it has fully engaged in marketing planning) and assessing whether there is an association between marketing planning and improved performance. To deal with the first issue, there is some consensus to suggest that a formal strategic plan should:

- consist of written plans
- cover more than one year of activity (and ideally three years)
- show awareness of alternative strategic options
- encompass shorter plans for major functional areas
- identify future resource requirements
- set out procedures for ongoing monitoring and modification
- include environmental (the business environment) scanning data.

COACHING SESSION 14

Identifying the important elements in a plan

Thinking about your organization or any situation where you have been involved in developing a plan, do you agree or disagree that your plan contained the elements listed?

Element	Strongly agree	Agree	Disagree	Strongly disagree
Consisted of written plans				
Covered more than one year of activity				
Had awareness of alternative strategic options				
Encompassed shorter plans for major functional areas				
Identified future resource requirements				
Encompassed procedures for ongoing monitoring and modification				
Included environmental scanning data				

STRATEGY AND TACTICS

The term 'strategic' (as in a formal strategic plan) or strategy is often used in planning. A dictionary definition of 'strategy' is as follows:

> 'in game theory, business theory, etc., a plan for successful action based on the rationality and interdependence of the moves of opposing or competing participants'.

This definition takes into consideration the 'moves' of others. In marketing, the key group of 'others' is competitors, i.e. 'opposing or competing' participants. However, for marketers, a key additional participant group is customers, with whom we are neither 'opposing' nor 'competing'. On first sight, these militaristic terms may seem to contradict the basic ethos of the marketing orientation described in Chapter 1, but they are used in this context because they reflect the nature of the process of deploying the organization's resources to achieve a defined objective.

It is useful to distinguish between **strategy** and **tactics**. We have both considered a dictionary definition of strategy and defined, from research evidence, the elements of strategy. Tactics are generally seen as the detail of strategy. For example, if we think about promotional strategy, we can see that strategic decisions would include defining the target audience, setting the key message themes (the message 'platform') and defining the main media that will reach the target audience. The tactical decisions would include the actual development of promotional messages and decisions about the timing of advertisements, etc.

Understanding this distinction is important because, if tactics are developed without a strategic overview, it is easy for decisions made in different areas of marketing – such as branding, pricing or promotional activity – to be in conflict. For example, if an organization decides to position a brand as a premium product and those responsible for advertising it decide that the key promotional message should be low price, such a conflict could seriously undermine the product's potential for success.

It is not that strategy is better than tactics, or vice versa. A rigorously developed strategy is no more than an academic exercise if it is not implemented and, clearly, tactical plans are central to such implementation. In addition, strategic plans tend to take a longer view – often three years – whereas tactical plans tend to be annual. There is a natural link between a three-year strategic plan and more detailed annual tactical plans.

The following model represents the relationship between strategy and tactics.

STRATEGIC

	Weak	Strong
TACTICAL Weak	Worst	Lacks implementation
TACTICAL Strong	Lacks direction	Best

Strategy and tactics matrix

The best outcome is obtained with both a strong strategic and a strong tactical focus. The worst outcome arises from a weak strategic and a weak tactical focus.

Where the organization has a strong strategic focus coupled with a weak tactical focus, there is a lack of implementation. Where the organization has a weak strategic focus and a strong tactical focus, there is a lack of direction.

The following case study illustrates the link between strategy and tactics. It shows how the strategy to increase customer satisfaction linked with one tactic to ensure that their products were easily available. (NB: there were several other tactics associated with this strategy.)

CASE STUDY: ZURICH FINANCIAL SERVICES GROUP

Zurich Financial Services Group (Zurich) is a global company that sells mainly business and personal insurance. It has a rich mix of products. Zurich employs over 60,000 people and operates in 170 countries.

Zurich's vision is 'to become the best global insurer as measured by our customers, our shareholders and our people'. To achieve this aim, Zurich is keen to add value and it does this by giving customers what they want, where and when they want it. The company aims for excellence in all its dealings with customers. All staff play a role in making sure that value is added and this means that teamwork and training are vital.

Since Zurich's *strategy* is to increase customer satisfaction, it carries out market research with over 7,000 customers to find out what they want. Using the findings, it puts resources where customers want most support. One *tactic* linked to this is to ensure that Zurich's products are easily available and to have the widest distribution footprint. This means having the largest presence in banks and other financial outlets and building strong links with financial intermediaries.

(Source and for the full case study: http://businesscasestudies.co.uk/zurich/a-customer-centred-approach-to-providing-insurance/strategy-and-tactics.html#axzz2VKWGMNHk)

♔♔ COACHING SESSION 15

Distinguishing between strategy and tactics

Consider the list of decisions in the table below.

In your opinion, which are more strategic and which are more tactical? Circle the appropriate number.

Decision	More strategic		← →	More tactical	
Deciding on the product features that carry benefits matched to customers' needs	3	2	1	2	3
Setting the range of products	3	2	1	2	3
Setting prices	3	2	1	2	3
Deciding on seasonal discounts	3	2	1	2	3
Selecting where products will be made available for purchase	3	2	1	2	3
Choosing where in the store to display the product	3	2	1	2	3
Defining the key promotional messages	3	2	1	2	3
Adapting promotional messages for different media	3	2	1	2	3

THE BENEFITS OF MARKETING PLANNING

It is probably becoming clear to you now that the process of marketing planning is quite demanding – in terms of both time and effort. Consequently, managers approaching the task of developing a marketing plan often ask themselves whether it's worth the effort.

Given the rate of change we experience, one could be excused for being sceptical about the benefits of marketing planning. Some writers suggest that organizations would be better served by adopting a more flexible, informal approach to developing marketing strategy. They argue that formal planning acts as a straightjacket that harms performance. At first sight this appears quite a reasonable view; however, research has shown this to be incorrect.

J. Scott Armstrong, Professor of Marketing at the University of Pennsylvania, conducted large meta-analyses of studies of the relationship between planning and performance. While he noted that there were problems with the way some organizations had implemented the planning process (not as completely as the standard model set out above would suggest) and differences in the way researchers had assessed the relationship between planning and performance, his final conclusion was as follows:

> '... despite problems with implementation and assessment, formal planning was associated with better performance in nearly **80 per cent** of the 42 studies and poorer performance in fewer than 8 per cent of them.'

(Source: http://ezinearticles.com/?Formal-Strategic-Planning--Does-it-Really-Help?&id=1241752)

This evidence is the fundamental reason for investing time and effort in marketing planning: there is a direct return on investment in the form of improved organizational performance.

Moreover, the discipline of marketing planning is directly linked to business survival – marketing planning helps organizations monitor their business environments and therefore isolate trends that may pose a significant threat. Theodore Levitt coined the term 'marketing myopia' in his seminal article published in the *Harvard Business Review* in 1960. Put simply, Levitt said that organizations must focus on customers' needs – *not* their product range. Marketing planning provides the process by which organizations can maintain a clear focus on their customers' needs and any threats that may come from current competitors, new entrants or substitute offerings.

Levitt took the US railroads as an example of an industry whose failure to grow was due to a limited market view. In 1960 the railroads were experiencing loss of revenue, not because the need for passenger transportation had declined or even because cars, aeroplanes and other modes of transport had filled that need. Rather, the industry was failing because senior executives saw themselves as 'in the railroad business' rather than the transportation business. They were railroad oriented instead of transportation oriented, product oriented instead of customer oriented.

 COACH'S TIP

Focus on customer needs

Organizations must focus primarily on customers' needs rather than on their products. In marketing planning, this means asking yourself how your product will benefit the customer rather than focusing on the features of the product itself.

THE PRACTICAL SIDE OF MARKETING PLANNING

Now we know that there is a significant body of evidence supporting the value of marketing planning as a discipline that aids managers in achieving their objectives, we need to focus on its practical nature. Below are some of the key factors to keep in mind when embarking on a marketing planning exercise in your organization.

- Marketing planning must be central to the way an organization engages with its marketplace. It cannot simply be a 'bolt-on' to the existing business structure.

- Similarly, an organization is not really engaged with marketing planning simply because the management says it is. The evidence for marketing planning in an organization is easy to see – detailed analysis, a clear focus on target market segments, a direct match of product benefits to customers' needs and a strategic focus on differentiating the business from the competition in the eyes of the customers – i.e. it is a set of *behaviours*.

- Marketing planning must be central to the way an organization is structured and part of the business 'culture' – the shared values and practices of all the employees.

- The introduction of marketing planning into an organization can be a powerful catalyst for change.

- The marketing plan is directly related to the corporate plan – and all other aspects of planning within the organization must link back to the marketing plan. The operational plan must be capable of delivering what we say is our differential advantage, the human resources plan must have the right people with the right skills and motivation to deliver what we say is our differential advantage and our financial plan must be able to provide the finance for us to implement our plan.

- There is a significant difference between a marketing plan and the commonly used 'business plan' format. The latter tends to be based on a broad description of what the business is all about, sometimes a subjective SWOT analysis and then a detailed treatment of projected cash-flow forecasts and profit & loss forecasts.

- Organizations might declare themselves committed to marketing planning and say they understand its discipline and value but, if management have failed to truly understand marketing planning, then the process becomes a chore – like completing your tax return – and something to be done as quickly as possible so that 'we can get back to the real work'. This situation will not deliver improved business performance.

- Marketing planning takes time to do and it takes time for the benefits to become apparent. In my own consulting experience, large organizations can take 12 months just to get to the point where those senior and middle managers understand the benefits of marketing planning, are clear about the stages in the process and are able to embark on a marketing planning exercise. Quite clearly, the benefits accrue some time after the plan has been implemented; so overall we have quite a long gestation period. In fact, one needs a plan for the plan!

- The marketing plan must embrace uncertainty about the near future, where there are a number of identifiable outcomes for which the organization must prepare. This means developing contingency plans based on the evidence available.

- The marketing plan must balance commitment and flexibility. Total commitment to a market or product provides the basis for a winning strategy, but commitment can make firms inflexible and therefore vulnerable to changes in the marketplace. A market-beating strategy will focus on just a few crucial high-commitment choices to be made now, while leaving flexibility for other such choices to be made over time.

 COACH'S TIP

Define your purpose

Marketing planning and leadership are inextricably linked. Defining what an organization will be, and why and to whom that will matter, is at the heart of a leader's role. It is the leader who says, 'This is our purpose, not that, this is who we will be; this is why our customers will prefer a world with us rather than without us.'

THE PITFALLS OF MARKETING PLANNING

We know that conducting a marketing planning exercise does not always deliver improved performance. In most cases this is because of one or more well-documented pitfalls. Below we set out some of the most common so that we can take steps to avoid them:

Ownership – it is important that those who have to implement the plan are given the opportunity to contribute to its development.

Senior management belief – senior management must believe that the process of planning will reduce risk in decision-making and contribute to the success of the business. Without this belief, the process can easily lose staff enthusiasm and rigour and it ultimately becomes a pointless bureaucratic exercise that is marginalized in the business.

Management buy-in – in addition to the need for senior management commitment, middle managers also have to believe in the value of marketing planning and be committed to its successful execution.

Management focus – managers are generally focused on today's issues – clearly their performance is measured on this. Marketing planning, as we have seen, is about future activities, and managers sometimes find it difficult to see the relevance of these issues today.

Delegation – because of the demands on line managers' time, some organizations choose to delegate the marketing planning exercise to a non-line manager. Often such individuals work at Head Office and are chosen because they have an MBA or similar qualification. Unfortunately, this approach rarely produces a plan that can deliver improved performance because of the lack of ownership by those managers who will have to implement it.

Human frailty – developing a marketing plan is an action conducted by humans and humans are susceptible to bias – over-optimism, loss aversion, confirmation bias (we look for evidence that confirms our previously held view), 'herding' (i.e. if all our colleagues say it, then it must be right), and champion bias (i.e. if the MD says it's right, then that's fine with us). Decisions must be evidence based, not personality based.

Ambiguity – since marketing and marketing planning can be a new area for some managers, a problem might be the ambiguity of the different terms used, which can cause a lack of confidence and disengagement with the planning process.

Company-wide appreciation – all employees need to appreciate the broad issues involved in the plan, so that they can contribute (i.e. share the same agendas as other staff) to its success.

Availability of appropriate resources – conducting a marketing planning exercise requires resources – mainly time and money. It is critically important that this is understood and that appropriate resources are made available for the exercise.

Poorly defined objectives – the objectives set for the marketing plan will define what the organization will do in the future. It is therefore critical that appropriate time and effort are deployed to ensure that the defined objectives are in line with the organization's goals and are realistic in terms of the marketplace.

Lack of rigour – The audit process (business and market) requires a significant amount of information, both from within the firm and from the marketplace. Lack of rigour in gathering, analysing and interpreting data can seriously undermine the effectiveness of the planning process. Managers need to obtain thorough and objective information to reduce risk in decision-making. It is also worth mentioning that modern IT systems and the planning process itself tend to produce a significant amount of information. Generally, 20 per cent of the information gathered accounts for 80 per cent of the information needed, so there is an additional need for selectivity.

Linking strategy and tactics – sometimes managers enthusiastically complete the planning process and lose sight of the need to implement the plan. This manifests itself as poorly drafted action plans and inadequate delegation of tasks.

Environmental sensitivity – marketers must guard against trying to 'fit' the world outside to the plan. Change is endemic to all market situations and planning processes must be reviewed in the light of the changing environment. Organizations must be environmentally sensitive and have the flexibility to be able to respond to changes, both opportunities and threats.

COACHING SESSION 16

Identifying the pitfalls

From the list above, consider the five potential pitfalls that you think are most important in terms of inhibiting your marketing plan.

Write them down here.

1 _____

_____

_____

2 _____

_____

_____

3 _____

_____

_____

4 _____

_____

_____

5 _____

_____

_____

COACHING SESSION 17

Avoiding the pitfalls

Now set our your ideas for how you are going to avoid the pitfalls you have identified in the coaching session above.

1 _____
_____
_____

2 _____
_____
_____

3 _____
_____
_____

4 _____
_____
_____

5 _____
_____
_____

NEXT STEPS

In this chapter we have:

- defined what marketing planning is and what it involves

- learned about the benefits of marketing planning for organizations

- looked at the practical side of effective marketing planning and the relationship between strategy and tactics

- explored the most common pitfalls in marketing planning and how to avoid them.

In the next chapter we are going to embark on the marketing planning process in more detail. The chapter will include an introduction to the key stages of the planning process and focus on the first stage: setting objectives. The coaching sessions will help you develop your qualitative and quantitative corporate and marketing objectives.

TAKEAWAYS

What have you learned about marketing planning that you didn't know before?

_____

_____

_____

_____

_____

_____

_____

_____

_____

_____

This chapter identified that marketing planning is more about management behaviour than simply managers saying that they engage with marketing planning. To what extent does your organization comply with this idea?

_____

_____

_____

_____

_____

_____

_____

_____

_____

_____

_____

Given that research shows that formal planning is associated with better performance, how could you use the research results comparing organizations using formal planning procedures with those that do not?

_____

_____

_____

_____

_____

_____

_____

_____

_____

What have you learned about the relationship between strategy and tactics and the key factors associated with marketing planning in practice?

_____

_____

_____

_____

_____

_____

_____

_____

_____

_____

What do you see as the most common pitfalls to effective marketing planning in your organization and how could you avoid them in your planning procedures?

_____

_____

_____

_____

_____

_____

_____

3

THE MARKETING PLANNING PROCESS AND SETTING OBJECTIVES

✔ OUTCOMES FROM THIS CHAPTER

- Understand the key stages in the marketing planning process.
- Make the link between corporate objectives and marketing objectives.
- Know how to begin the process of setting marketing objectives.

KEY STAGES IN THE MARKETING PLANNING PROCESS

Marketing planning is a logical and objective way of deciding how to marshal and direct the resources of the organization. It may be seen as a series of key steps or stages, starting with the setting of objectives and ending with the implementing and monitoring of the plan.

The following flow chart summarizes the process.

The marketing planning process

The flow chart describes a series of interrelated activities that form the basis of the marketing planning process. In brief, the stages of the process are:

1. **Set objectives**

   Create a set of marketing objectives that is generally quantitative (e.g. turnover, profitability, market share) for the planning period and strongly linked to the corporate objectives of the organization.

2. **Business audit**

   Review the strengths and weaknesses of the organization; in essence this is a review of 'where we are now and where we have come from'.

3. **Market audit**

   Review the opportunities and threats in the marketplace, including analysis of customers and competitors and the broader market 'environment' (i.e. PEST factors).

4. **The 'targeting' exercise**

   Match the organization's strengths to opportunities in the marketplace so that the firm can obtain the best return on effort, producing a series of target market segments.

5. **Define the marketing strategy**

   Decide what to produce, how much to charge, where the customer will buy the product, and how to inform and persuade the customer to buy the product.

6. **Implementation**

   Develop action plans that set operational variables, establish time limits and deadlines, communicate and assign tasks, develop sales forecasts, determine action plans for individuals and prepare budgets.

7. **Monitoring**

   Compare actual performance with planned and, where there are deficiencies, take action to put the plan 'back on track'.

The process culminates in a marketing plan – for most organizations this means a written document. The two broad aspects of marketing planning are therefore:

- the *process* of planning
- the *written plan*.

The process helps managers focus on key aspects of their organization and the marketplace(s) in which they operate. The written plan provides the basis for implementing the actions necessary to achieve the goals of the organization. In addition, the written plan helps disseminate the thinking behind the plan across the organization, enabling co-workers to place their roles within the broader planning framework.

One might say that there are two broad elements to marketing planning – thinking and doing.

COACH'S TIP

'Think slowly, act quickly.'

This ancient Greek proverb extols the virtue of taking time to weigh up the options before acting, but stresses the need to carry out the selected strategy without delay. Thinking helps us reduce the risk in deciding what we should do and therefore significantly improves the probability of success. This simple proverb encapsulates the value of marketing planning for an organization.

To start the process, we need to focus on our objectives.

THE LINK BETWEEN CORPORATE AND MARKETING OBJECTIVES

It is worth spending time to examine the differences between corporate and marketing objectives.

Corporate objectives encapsulate the purpose and nature of the organization – it is what brings the business into being. It is a desire to use resources available to the organization, such as human, financial and technological, to achieve a stated goal or reach a defined destination. An organization's mix of resources can be thought of as the capabilities of the organization. To achieve the organization's goal, these capabilities must deliver something that customers want and that can be differentiated from what other providers offer.

Defining a corporate objective may sound straightforward but it can actually be quite difficult to do in practice. For instance, the owner of a chain of coffee shops might define its corporate objective as 'to become the market leader in the coffee shops market in our geographical area'. In setting such an objective, the management would need to define:

- their geographical area – is it a city or a region, or a number of regions?
- what they mean by 'market leader' – does this mean, for example, having the largest £ value of sales in the area compared with their competitors (market share), or the fastest growth in turnover compared with their competitors, or the highest level of customer satisfaction compared with their competitors?

- the 'market' – is it based on *all* outlets that sell coffee? For example, it might refer only to cafeterias in retail outlets/public transport hubs, independent coffee shops or multinational branded chains.

Defining one's market is important when defining realistic and achievable corporate objectives. In addition, large businesses (especially plcs) have to meet the needs of their shareholders and generally this translates into annual dividends and share value appreciation. In fact, corporate governance is concerned with the sustainability of an enterprise.

There are seven measures of sustainability:

1. Profitable growth

2. Health and safety

3. Environmental impact

4. Ethical conduct

5. Employment rights

6. Human rights

7. Community engagement.

Marketing objectives, on the other hand, are concerned with achieving defined outcomes in terms of those variables specific to marketing (i.e. customers and markets). Marketing objectives are the 'deliverables' that a marketing plan would be designed to produce. Given that the marketing activity is the main interface between the organization and the marketplace (particularly customers), it follows that the marketing objectives must be closely aligned with corporate objectives.

The ultimate aim of marketing is to match benefits to customer needs, so the universal marketing objective (for private sector businesses, at least) must be to achieve sales. However, making a sale and creating or keeping a customer can be thought of as the last stage in the marketing process and several other, related objectives will need to be included.

In addition, we have seen the relationship between strategy and tactics and, in effect, the organization's corporate objectives translate through the strategic marketing objectives into the tactical marketing objectives:

Corporate objectives (medium to long term)

↓

Strategic marketing objectives (medium term – normally three years)

↓

Tactical marketing objectives (short term – normally one year)

Marketing objectives include things like:

- sales levels for the organization
- sales levels for particular products
- sales growth
- profit on sales
- market share
- customer awareness and disposition to our product.

Managers are used to focusing on targets, often expressed as numbers – a 10-per-cent increase in total sales on last year's figures, for example. I have worked as a consultant with a wide range of client organizations and witnessed managers taking a very rudimentary view of setting marketing objectives. They approach the exercise as a 'task and finish' activity (i.e. we will fill in the necessary boxes on the form and move on) and this prevents them from fully appreciating the strategic implications of what they have to do. It is important to avoid simple form filling, which discourages thought about strategy.

It is important, when setting marketing objectives, to consider the mechanism that delivers the objective. For example, an increase in sales of existing products must come from either current customers buying more of our product or new customers buying the product for the first time. In marketing terms, this situation represents two distinct market segments that require different marketing strategies.

 COACH'S TIP

Sell benefits, not products

Fundamentally, managers have to deliver benefits matched to customer needs to achieve the increase in sales – it is about matching benefits to customer needs, not matching customers to our products.

SETTING MARKETING OBJECTIVES

Generally, setting objectives will start with a description of a series of qualitative objectives (such as a mission statement) that provides a platform of corporate objectives upon which the marketing objectives can be built. These qualitative objectives will need to be 'operationalized' (i.e. made quantitative) so that performance against these objectives can be measured. Ultimately, objectives are defined in quantitative terms.

Here are some examples of marketing objectives:

- To achieve market 'leadership' (to be specified) in a defined market/segment
- To achieve 60 per cent of defined market perceiving our brand to be 'the best'
- To achieve 10-per-cent growth in turnover on the previous year
- To achieve a 45-per-cent share of defined market
- To improve operating profit from 15 to 20 per cent.

There are two important points to remember:

1. These objectives will be the basis for developing the strategic direction of the organization and will involve the commitment of corporate resources (i.e. money and time). What we aim for here will have a profound effect on the future of the business. All other functional plans (such as operational, human resources and financial) will be built upon what we decide here.

2. We must consider these objectives in the context of the business and market audits (discussed in detail later in the workbook). The business audit will identify strengths and weaknesses in the organization and the market audit will include customers (segmented on some dimension), competitors, intermediaries, suppliers, the political framework, the economic framework, the societal framework and the technological framework. Therefore we must assess how realistic these objectives are in terms of what is possible, given market conditions. For example, it would be unrealistic for a small business with access to limited capital to set an objective to be the world market leader in building nuclear power stations within 12 months!

Let's think about how different types of organization might approach setting down their objectives. A division of a large business or a medium-sized business will probably have some well-defined corporate objectives. In addition, plcs have to meet the needs of their shareholders and generally this translates into annual dividends and share value appreciation. As we have seen, the objectives for the marketing plan must respond to these corporate objectives.

Smaller owner-managed and start-up businesses may also have established corporate objectives but they are also likely to focus on the needs of the principal/s. These needs are likely to be broader than just economic needs, and include lifestyle issues that will need to be taken into consideration.

Not-for-profit organizations will not necessarily have only economic objectives (such as turnover or surplus of income over expenditure targets) as their corporate objectives. They will consequently need to develop their marketing planning objectives differently. For instance, a charity set up to help ex-service personnel to re-enter civilian life might set its objectives in terms of the number of ex-service personnel it will support and the type of support it will deliver during the planning period.

! COACH'S TIP

See marketing objectives in context

We must remember that one cannot define marketing objectives in isolation – market forces have a major impact on what can realistically be achieved.

CASE STUDY

XYZ Construction Ltd*

*This is a real business but its identity has been disguised for reasons of commercial confidentiality.

XYZ Construction is a construction and engineering business operating across a number of regions in the UK. The business has enjoyed significant growth, mainly from its core areas but also from winning major projects outside its core areas. The firm has won a big contract in a region where they had previously had no presence and the Board sees this as an ideal opportunity to use this 'flywheel' project to build a regional business. They have promoted a successful regional manager to take responsibility for the new major contract and included in his job description the objective of establishing a profitable ongoing presence in the new region. As part of this, they have charged him with developing a marketing plan to support the establishment of the new regional business.

Below is the list of qualitative objectives he has developed for the new region's marketing plan:

- To establish a sustainable business unit in the new region
- To ensure the successful completion of the major contract
- To achieve budget turnover and operating profit targets
- To establish XYZ as a serious competitor in the new region
- To establish strategic relationships with key personnel aligned to the regional market.

He then translates this list of qualitative objectives into quantitative objectives, i.e. objectives that will allow measurement of 'actual' (what is achieved) against 'plan' (what was set out as the objectives).

Qualitative objective	Measured by (quantitative objective)
To establish a sustainable business unit in the new region	• New regional office to be fully functional by Month 5, Year 1
To ensure the successful completion of the major contract	• Operating profit on completed contract to meet or exceed budget margin • Client satisfaction against satisfaction criteria • To score on average 8 (out of 10)
To achieve budget turnover (TO) and operating profit (OP) targets	• TO measured in £ million • OP measured as % of TO
To establish XYZ as a serious competitor in the new region	• To achieve 60% favourable disposition from decision-makers in region (sector market research) • To obtain bid opportunities on 50% of 'of interest' projects in the region
To establish strategic relationships with key personnel aligned to the regional market	• 50% awareness and 25% favourable disposition of decision-makers in region (sector market research) • Engagement with decision-makers in top 20% of client businesses in region (client relationship management)

Let us consider some of the points arising from this case study:

■ The qualitative objectives include a mix of reasonably 'hard' objectives (such as turnover and operating profit targets, which will be drawn from the corporate objectives for the business as a whole) along with 'softer', more indirect objectives such as decision-maker attitudes.

■ The second qualitative objective can be seen as an operational management issue – the successful completion of the major contract. This is included in the list of marketing objectives because creating a satisfied customer is central to marketing and this 'flywheel' project is central to the establishment of the new regional business.

■ There will be a need to produce unambiguous definitions of terms used – for example, what do we mean by 'serious' competitor in the region and by 'strategic relationships with key personnel aligned to the regional market'?

■ The second stage of quantifying the qualitative objectives will start to deal with some of the ambiguities and will also define how we are going to measure performance (i.e. actual against planned).

■ Some qualitative objectives convert into more than one quantitative objective.

Now you need to develop your own objectives for your plan.

COACHING SESSION 18

Your qualitative objectives

Write down your own list of qualitative objectives for your marketing plan.

1 _____
_____
_____

2 _____
_____
_____

3 _____
_____
_____

4 _____
_____
_____

5 _____
_____
_____

6 _____
_____
_____

COACHING SESSION 19

Your quantitative objectives

Write down your quantitative objectives – objectives that can be measured – for your marketing plan.

Qualitative objective	Measured by (quantitative objective)

→ NEXT STEPS

In this chapter we have:

- looked at the seven key stages of the marketing planning process

- identified that there are two broad aspects to marketing planning: thinking and doing

- considered the nature of corporate objectives – the purpose and nature of the organization

- looked at the differences between corporate and marketing objectives and the links between them

- examined the process of setting marketing objectives.

In the next chapter we will explain the nature and purpose of the business audit – to review the strengths and weaknesses of the organization. This analysis provides half the evidence necessary to make decisions regarding the best match of organizational capabilities with market opportunities (which will be analysed through the market audit).

TAKEAWAYS

Now that you understand the seven key stages of the marketing planning process – set objectives, business audit, market audit, the 'targeting' exercise, defining the marketing strategy, implementation and monitoring – you can begin to assess how they have been addressed in your organization. Are any of them missing and, if so, can you take steps to include them?

_____

_____

_____

_____

_____

_____

_____

_____

You have considered the nature of corporate objectives (i.e. the purpose and nature of the organization) and marketing objectives (i.e. achieving defined outcomes in terms of the variables specific to marketing – customers and markets). In your organization, how are the distinctions as well as the links made between them?

_____

_____

_____

_____

_____

_____

_____

_____

What thoughts do you now have about the process of setting marketing objectives in your organization? Would it be useful to start from a qualitative articulation of objectives and then translate these into quantitative, measurable targets upon which a strategy can be based and measured?

_____

_____

_____

_____

_____

_____

_____

_____

_____

_____

What else have you learned from reading this chapter that could be of practical help to you?

_____

_____

_____

_____

_____

_____

_____

_____

_____

_____

_____

_____

4 THE BUSINESS AUDIT

- Understand strengths and weaknesses, opportunities and threats by doing a SWOT analysis of the organization.
- Know about organizational capabilities and competitive advantage.
- Make the link between the marketing audit and the business audit.
- Know how to conduct a business audit.

HOW TO DO A SWOT ANALYSIS

The analysis stage of the marketing planning process includes the business audit, which is a review of the nature of your organization. An element of this is the SWOT analysis, which refers to:

- the **s**trengths and **w**eaknesses within your organization
- the **o**pportunities and **t**hreats within your business environment.

Assessing the **s**trengths and **w**eaknesses within your organization and the **o**pportunities and **t**hreats within your business environment (which we will consider further in Chapters 5–7) can provide you with a sound basis upon which you can build your marketing plan. For instance, the best return on effort will derive from *matching* your organization's strengths to opportunities in the marketplace. Let's consider each element in turn.

Assessing your organization

Strengths are the positive attributes, tangible and intangible, of your organization. They can come from a range of sources, including control of scarce materials (e.g. minerals), patents, economies of scale (in manufacturing), human resources (skills, knowledge, experience), availability of finance, brand strength or customer loyalty.

Weaknesses are the negative attributes of the organization. They can arise from the same sources as strengths, but in a negative format. One key point about weaknesses is that, because they arise within your organization, they do fall within your control and so you may be able to address some of them and convert them into strengths.

Assessing your business environment

Opportunities are positive factors in the business environment. In the first instance, they derive from customers (their current perceived needs, unfulfilled or poorly met needs) and the weaknesses of competitors. Changes in the wider business environment can also produce opportunities that the organization can exploit – for example, changes to legislation such as the Climate Change Act (political), changes in economic factors such as unemployment levels (economic), changes in social attitudes and norms such as attitudes to smoking (societal), and changes in technology such as mobile communications technology (technological).

Threats are negative factors in the business environment. They can arise from the same sources as opportunities: for example, changing customer perceived needs might mean that our offering is no longer seen as the best match to their needs; or improvements in competitor offerings could make theirs more attractive to customers.

Using a SWOT analysis

A SWOT analysis can be seen as a snapshot of an organization's position at a given point in time. Given that our plan is committed to action in the future, we must take account of changes occurring both in our business environment and within our organization. For instance, are our patents due to run out soon? Are key executives due to retire soon?

The SWOT analysis is a deceptively simple tool, but very powerful if conducted with rigour and acted on. In practice, managers often display limited analysis, a subjective (rather than objective) focus, bias based on personal preferences and lack of preparedness to reinvent the business in the face of hard evidence for the need to do so – because of changes in the marketplace. In Chapter 2 we looked at Theodore Levitt's famous *Harvard Business Review* article, 'Marketing myopia' and his example of the US railroads. SWOT analysis and the will to act upon the findings would have made the railroads more competitive in a changing business environment.

ORGANIZATIONAL CAPABILITIES AND COMPETITIVE ADVANTAGE

As already stated, marketing planning seeks to apply a logical and objective approach to deciding how an organization's *capabilities* will be matched to opportunities in the marketplace so that the objectives of the organization can be met. Organizational capabilities are the sum of our strengths (such as those listed above), which provide a compelling proposition to our customers. Where this mix of attributes and resources enables the organization to perform at a higher level than others in the same sector, this is described as 'competitive advantage'. It has been said that, if you know where your competitive advantage comes from, then you know where your profit comes from.

True competitive advantage comes from:

- **market position** – where a company is dominant in a market and its dominance provides a competitive advantage

- **special capabilities** – the things a company does well, such as innovating or managing customer relationships, patenting a product or controlling scarce minerals.

Too often, managers are subjective and over-optimistic when claiming special capabilities. A special capability must be central to an organization's performance and be possessed by the organization and not its competitors. Let's take the UK supply of **aggregates** as an example. Aggregates include sand, gravel and crushed stone, and they are used in the construction industry. The Office of Fair Trading, in its review of the sector published in August 2011, estimated that there were some 235 operators supplying primary aggregates from more than 1,200 sites including quarries and wharves. The top five companies together accounted for 73 per cent of total production. The top three – Tarmac, Aggregate Industries and Hanson – together accounted for 53 per cent of the market. These three companies have a special capability based on the control of a scarce mineral.

Special capabilities are often specific in nature and difficult to obtain (because everyone wants them). Managers can be lulled into a false sense of security by mistaking the size of their business for a scale advantage or conclude that they have special capabilities simply by comparing their business performance with that of their competitors, when that superior performance might arise from another source, such as positional advantage or just simple good luck.

CASE STUDY: IMI

IMI is a global engineering group involving many different engineering specialities. It is recognized worldwide for its innovation, expertise and global service, selling engineering solutions in over 50 countries to match customer needs. IMI's competitive advantage comes from combining the knowledge and skills of its people with an in-depth understanding of what its customers want and need. IMI's strengths of expertise and innovation differentiate it in the markets it serves.

IMI operates in a B2B (business-to-business) environment, providing tailored products and services to companies. Clients include large household names such as Chevron, Shell, Volvo Trucks, General Motors, Coca-Cola and McDonalds, as well as smaller niche companies dealing in specialized equipment or building materials.

IMI's strategy brings together three key aspects:

- its engineering skills in fluid technology and innovation

- its market-leading positions in its chosen niche markets

- its exposure to markets that are benefiting from long-term structural growth trends such as climate change and urbanization.

IMI calls the point of overlap between these three factors the 'sweet spot'. Where these three areas come together is known as strategic convergence. It is an area where IMI expects to achieve clear market leadership, higher profit margins, greater product differentiation, and opportunities to meet global trends and to grow. Over half of IMI's operations are positioned within the strategic 'sweet spot' today, with plans to increase this to over 70 per cent over the next five years.

Using a powerful combination of knowledge, skills and market insight enables IMI not only to develop innovative solutions for its customers but also to create a competitive advantage.

IMI's strategy of 'engineering advantage' enables it to support its customers in niche markets across the globe in a responsible way. It brings together the company's values, expertise and knowledge in order to meet the challenges of the global drivers it has identified. Its strategy brings together its people and processes to maximize the capabilities of the business, provide more value for customers and make the organization distinctive.

(Source and for the full case study: http://businesscasestudies.co.uk/imi/engineering-advantage-strategy-in-action/introduction.html#ixzz2W7S8QpCe)

IMI's competitive advantage comes from *special capabilities* – from the knowledge and skills of its people and the in-depth understanding of its customers' needs.

⏻⏻ COACHING SESSION 20

Your competitive advantage

Consider the factors that you think provide your organization with a competitive advantage.

Write them in the space below or, if you can't think of any, write down the factors that you think could be developed to provide one. Start with the most important.

1 _____

2 _____

3 _____

4 _____

5 _____

HOW THE MARKET AUDIT LINKS TO THE BUSINESS AUDIT

Auditing can be defined as a systematic and independent examination of data, statements, records, operations and performances (financial or otherwise) of an organization for a stated purpose. Audits are used in a wide range of management situations, such as the quality audit. Probably the best-known audit is the financial audit conducted by independent auditors to meet the requirements of company legislation, such as the Companies Acts in the UK. The audit covers an income statement (profit & loss), a statement of the financial position (balance sheet) and a statement of cash flow. This report is filed at Companies House in the UK. In the USA different states have different rules. For more information, see: http://www.world-stock-exchanges.net/usa.html

The market audit

A market audit (which we will consider in more detail later) is a comprehensive, systematic, periodic evaluation of an organization's marketing capabilities. The audit examines the goals, strategies and processes of the marketing function as well the personnel involved. The market audit focuses on what we currently do, such as our product, price, distribution and promotional activities. Fundamentally, we want to answer the question, 'How do we create satisfied customers?'

Management consultants often perform a *management survey* as the first stage in a consulting assignment. The following model describes the management consultants' approach to the management survey:

Past, present, future – state of client affairs

↓

Strengths and weaknesses

↓

Possible improvements

↓

Action needed and help proposed

(Source: *Management Consulting, a guide to the profession*, edited by M. Kubr, International Labour Office, Geneva, 4th ed. 2002)

The management survey covers a wide range of topics, including:

1. the client's organization
2. the environment (which we will cover as part of the market audit)

3. input resources

4. objectives, policies and plans (overall)

5. detailed surveys of the objectives, policies and plans, activities and performance of the key organizational functions:

    i   Finance

    ii   Marketing

    iii Production (Operations)

    iv Research & Development

    v   Personnel (Human Resources)

    vi overall organizational performance

    vii management and organizational structure.

The business audit

The business audit takes a holistic view of the organization to assess its strengths and weaknesses from the point of view of the marketplace. This involves taking the key approach of the marketing audit and including some of the components from the general management survey. The overarching consideration is to produce an objective picture of where the organization is now and where it has come from. We are concerned with those positive attributes (strengths) that can be *matched* to opportunities in the market place and those negative attributes (weaknesses) that we can rank in terms of importance to the competitive position of the organization and that can be *converted* from a weakness into a strength.

COACH'S TIP

Remember…

The business audit constitutes only half of the analysis necessary to make judgements about what has to be done – the other half, of course, is the marketing audit. The business audit therefore incorporates the marketing audit and takes a broader view that includes the key issues associated with the nature of the organization. It has at its centre the question, 'What is/are our competitive advantage/s?'

CONDUCTING A BUSINESS AUDIT

The business audit has four distinct stages:

1. A review of recent performance

2. A review of the marketing mix

3. Senior management's perceptions of the organization's strengths and weaknesses

4. Consolidation of key strengths and weaknesses.

A review of recent performance

To start the business audit, we need to review the recent performance of the organization. For most organizations the two key measures of performance are turnover and profitability.

Turnover is reasonably straightforward to define: it is the value of goods and/or services sold during a defined period such as a financial year. Clearly, there may be a difference between when a sale is made and when payment is received – in business-to-business markets, for example, payment can be 30+ days following the sale date. Complications can also arise when dealing with part payments on large contracts, such as in the construction and engineering sectors, where contract values can be very large and delivery can be over a long time period. For instance, the build cost of the London Olympics 2012 was in the region of £5 billion. In such cases, turnover is based on the value of work carried out during the period (for example, the financial year).

Profit is more difficult to define: for instance, it might be net profit after tax, net profit before tax or gross profit. Given that we want to measure the performance of the business, it would be valuable for us to take a measure of profitability that is directly comparable from product to product and period to period. The best definition of profit for us is **contribution** or gross profit – i.e. the sales value less total variable (also known as direct) costs. Variable costs include materials and direct labour, i.e. those costs that increase when we make more products and decrease when we make fewer products.

Let's look at an example of drawing strengths and weaknesses from turnover and contribution data. The two tables below present turnover and contribution figures by product and market segment for company ABC Ltd. (These data are based on a real business but some of the figures have been changed to protect the company's identity.)

Company ABC Ltd: turnover and contribution data by product, 2010–12

Turnover £000s					
Product	2010	2011	2012	Total	% change 2012 on 2010
1	4,705	4,078	5,062	13,845	7.6
2	5,803	3,061	665	9,529	−88.5
3	27,264	29,884	14,171	71,319	−48.0
4	15,787	3,959	5,939	25,685	−62.4
5	11,863	8,294	12,594	32,751	6.2
Total	65,422	49,276	38,431	153,129	−41.3
Contribution £000s					
1	448	847	1,154	2,449	157.6
2	730	706	47	1,483	−93.6
3	2,611	3,960	1,814	8,385	−30.5
4	1,918	888	672	3,478	−65.0
5	783	774	1,808	3,365	130.9
Total	6,490	7,175	5,495	19,160	−15.3
% contribution to turnover					
1	9.5	20.8	22.8	17.7	139.4
2	12.6	23.1	7.1	15.6	−43.8
3	9.6	13.3	12.8	11.8	33.7
4	12.1	22.4	11.3	13.5	−6.9
5	6.6	9.3	14.4	10.3	117.5
Total	9.9	14.6	14.3	12.5	44.1

Company ABC Ltd: turnover and contribution data by segment, 2010–12

Turnover £000s					
Segment	2010	2011	2012	Total	% change 2012 on 2010
A	13,235	1,798	4621	19,654	−65.1
B	44,431	33,424	31,988	109,843	−28.0
C	5,761	9,478	1,505	16,744	−73.9
D	1,995	4,576	317	6,888	−84.1
Total	65,422	49,276	38,431	153,129	−41.3

Contribution £000s					
A	366	114	−35	445	−109.6
B	4,506	4,945	5,068	14,519	12.5
C	1,423	1,462	297	3,182	−79.1
D	195	654	165	1,014	−15.4
Total	6,490	7,175	5,495	19,160	−15.3
% contribution to turnover					
A	2.8	6.3	−0.8	2.3	−127.4
B	10.1	14.8	15.8	13.2	56.2
C	24.7	15.4	19.7	19.0	−20.1
D	9.8	14.3	52.1	14.7	432.5
Total	9.9	14.6	14.3	12.5	44.1

COACHING SESSION 21

Using data to analyse strengths and weaknesses

Study the data about ABC Ltd that is given in the two tables above.

Write down below four strengths of the company that you can draw from the turnover and contribution data.

1 _____

2 _____

3 _____

4 _____

Now write down below the four weaknesses of the company that you can draw from the turnover and contribution data.

1 _____

2 _____

3 _____

4 _____

Appendix 2 presents some more examples of strengths and weaknesses drawn from turnover and contribution data. Compare your findings here with those set out in Appendix 2. Note them below.

1 _____

2 _____

3 _____

4 _____

5 _____

6 _____

7 _____

8 _____

When total turnover declines by 40 per cent over two years, this has to be seen as a significant problem and management would want to look at the reasons behind this decline.

However, in our example, contribution declined much less significantly and this is encouraging. Clearly, the analysis leads us to ask further questions and 'drill' more deeply into the data to understand the underlying reasons so that appropriate action can be taken. These are some of the questions we might ask:

- Why has turnover declined by 40 per cent over three years? Has the market declined at a similar rate?

- Particularly, why has turnover declined so severely for Products 2 and 4? Do they no longer meet customers' needs?

- Why has turnover in Segment C declined so severely?

- Why has contribution in Segment B increased and can we reverse the drop in turnover in this segment?

In its analysis of turnover and contribution, our example is quite limited. Often, organizations also study geographical turnover and contribution data, they analyse the top ten customers by turnover and they review associated contribution levels. In addition, a wide range of accounting ratios can be used to help understand the strengths and weaknesses of the organization.

For instance, we can look at:

- **Productivity**

  This is turnover divided by numbers of employees.

- **Return on capital employed (ROCE)**

  Capital employed is fixed assets + current assets – current liabilities. ROCE is a measure of the returns that a company is realizing from its capital, an important indicator of how efficiently a business is being managed.

- **Current ratio**

  This is current assets divided by current liabilities multiplied by 100. This ratio looks at assets available to pay liabilities falling soon and is a measure of liquidity.

 COACH'S TIP

Find out more

For more information about business ratio analysis, visit the following Institute of Chartered Accountants in England & Wales site:

http://www.bized.co.uk/compfact/ratios/index.htm

There are two more important points to make about measuring business performance for marketing planning:

1. Financial reporting and management accounting systems do not always gather and manipulate data relevant to marketing decision-making. Modern accounting software systems should be able to provide reports relevant to the kind of analysis we have looked at in the above example. However, if the key variable data are not collected (i.e. type of product, type of customer/market segment, etc.) then clearly this is not possible. Sometimes changes must be made to recording transactions to allow analysis of turnover and contribution for marketing decision-making.

2. This type of analysis can generate a significant amount of data but it is worth remembering that the Pareto rule applies here – 20 per cent of the data provides 80 per cent of the information we use to reduce risk in decision-making. While it is worth experimenting with analysis, ultimately we will focus on a relatively small number of key 'metrics' that form the core of identifying strengths and weaknesses.

A review of the marketing mix

The next stage of the business audit focuses on the marketing mix. Again our aim is to isolate strengths and weaknesses, this time in the marketing mix.

We can base our review on a series of questions about the customer, the product, the price, the channels and promotion.

Customer

- How do current and potential customers rate us in terms of meeting their needs, reputation, product quality, service and after-sales and price?

- How do groups (segments) of customers make their buying decisions?

- What do we know about how customers' needs are changing?

Product

- Do the features and benefits in our products match the perceived needs of the target customers?

- Is the *width* (how many products we have, e.g. two-seater sports cars, four-door family cars, luxury saloons, SUVs) and *depth* (differentiation within width of range, e.g. engine type/size, trim/equipment levels) of our product range matched to the needs of the target customer segments?

- Are there any products that should be phased out?

- Are there new products that should be added?

- Are there any products that should be revised (e.g. quality, features, or style improvements)?

Price

- Are prices set on sound cost, demand and competitive criteria?

- Do the customers see our price/s as being in line with their perceived value for this offering?

- Do we use price promotions effectively?

Channels

- What are our distribution objectives and strategies? (Do we want to be in the same channels as our competitors or do we want to use alternative channels?)

- Is there adequate market coverage and service support?

- Should we consider changing our degree of reliance on intermediaries (distributors, retailers, etc.) and consider more direct channels such as the Internet?

Promotion

- What are our current promotional activities?

- What are the budgets/spend levels for our promotional tools (e.g. advertising, press relations, mail, outlets, personal selling, Internet)?

- What are our core messages and are they in line with matching our product benefits to customer perceived needs?

- What are the results of our evaluation of the effectiveness of our promotional activities?

Management's perceptions of the organization's strengths and weaknesses

Since the management of an organization is both a key asset and a prime source of knowledge, the business audit needs to include direct questioning of management to capture their experiences, knowledge and understanding. Some organizations prefer to use someone from outside the organization for this exercise, simply because they are emotionally detached and less likely to introduce any interviewer bias.

The method adopted could include direct face-to-face questioning or a focus-group setting. Do not limit the interviews to senior management; often middle and lower management are closer to the customer and can offer important insights. The content of the interview or focus group should cover:

- perceptions of the company's strengths and weaknesses

- perceptions of customers' perceived needs (perceptions of value, benefits at price)

- perceptions of the competition's strengths and weaknesses (market/segment shares, capabilities, geographical coverage, business objectives, policies, strategies, etc.)

- perceptions of the PEST (political, economic, societal and technological) environment in which the business operates.

COACH'S TIP

Structure the exercise

To provide structure to this consultation exercise, it is advisable to divide it into sections and ask management to consider strengths and weaknesses in the four functional areas of the organization: marketing, operations, HR and finance.

Consolidation of key strengths and weaknesses

We have considered the Pareto rule as applied to the relationship between information and data. To get the best value out of the business audit, the final step is to produce a consolidated list of key strengths and weaknesses. This list will be based on the three preceding stages described above:

- A review of recent performance

- A review of the marketing mix

- Senior management's perceptions of the organization's strengths and weaknesses.

To compile the list, the first step is to look for themes (both strengths and weaknesses) that occur in one or more of the business audit stages. The next step is to assess the relative importance of these isolated themes in terms of meeting the organization's corporate objectives. This assessment must be based on judgement but it is often quite easy to isolate the key themes, simply by their very nature.

 COACH'S TIP

Look at the five key behaviours

Chapter 1 listed the five key behaviours of organizations that effectively (and profitably) make the customer/marketing orientation the operational basis of their businesses. It is worth taking a second look at that list when thinking about your business audit: they are market sensing, quality focus, internal marketing, adaptive response and external relationships.

When you have completed your consolidated list, it may be worth comparing it with the list you constructed for Coaching session 4 in Chapter 1.

Any work associated with future decision-making must take account of the fact that we live in a constantly changing world – in the last 100 years we have witnessed a geometric rate of change (political, economic, societal and technological). As the Greek philosopher Heraclitus put it, 'The only constant is change.' We will return to this issue later in the book.

COACHING SESSION 22

Your business audit

You now need to conduct your own business audit based on the four stages described above.

1. Your review of recent performance:

2. Your review of the marketing mix:

3. Senior management's perceptions of the organization's strengths and weaknesses:

4. Your consolidated list of key strengths and weaknesses:

 ONLINE RESOURCE

Turnover and contribution table

Download a table from this website:

www.TYCoachbooks.com/Marketingplanning

 NEXT STEPS

In this chapter we have:

- looked at the value of SWOT analysis and at the relationship between organizational capabilities and competitive advantage

- looked at the link between the market audit and the business audit

- guided you through the four stages of the business audit so that you can complete one for your own organization.

The next chapter continues our focus on the analysis stage of the marketing planning process and begins to look at the second part of the SWOT analysis, the market audit. This is the assessment of the opportunities and threats that exist in the business environment in which we operate. The first stage is to look at customers and potential customers. Later chapters will focus on competitors and the broader business environment – the marketplace.

TAKEAWAYS

Are you clear about how to apply a SWOT analysis to your organization in order to conduct a business audit? When you looked at the strengths and weaknesses within your organization and the opportunities and threats within your business environment, what new knowledge did you gain?

_____

_____

_____

_____

_____

_____

_____

_____

How do you think your organization's capabilities (the sum of its strengths) relate to its competitive advantage (the mix of attributes and resources that enables it to perform at a higher level than others in the same sector)?

_____

_____

_____

_____

_____

_____

_____

_____

_____

_____

Now that you have considered the link between the market audit (a comprehensive, systematic, periodic evaluation of an organization's marketing capabilities) and the business audit (which takes a holistic view of the organization to assess its strengths and weaknesses from the point of view of the marketplace), how will you use this information in your own context?

_____

_____

_____

_____

_____

_____

_____

_____

_____

Have you gone through the four stages of a business audit using the method set out in this chapter? If there are gaps, what do you plan to do to fill them?

_____

_____

_____

_____

_____

_____

_____

_____

_____

5 THE MARKET AUDIT: CUSTOMERS

 OUTCOMES FROM THIS CHAPTER

- Understand why customers buy.
- Appreciate how (and why) customers can be 'segmented' into different customer groups.
- Recognize how customers select from different options.
- Know where to obtain information on customers to help in the marketing planning process.

WHY DO CUSTOMERS BUY?

Before we can answer the question 'Why do customers buy?' we first have to ask 'Who are our customers?' As we have seen, at first sight this might seem a simple question, with the answer, 'Our customers are the people who buy our products or services.' However, customers come in many types: they can be individuals and families, small and medium-sized businesses, public limited companies (plcs) and even government departments.

It is possible, therefore, to divide customers into two broad markets:

- **consumer markets** – e.g. individuals and families
- **organizational or business-to-business (B2B) markets** – e.g. businesses, not-for-profit/chartable organizations and government departments.

To understand why customers buy, we have to look at customers' motives, values and attitudes.

Motives

At the heart of a perceived need is a driver, a motive. Abraham Maslow produced a hierarchical structure of needs based on five core levels.

Maslow's hierarchy of needs

Level	Motive	Need
Lower level	Physiological	Water, sleep, food
	Safety	Security, shelter, protection
	Belongingness	Love, friendship, acceptance by others
	Ego needs	Prestige, status, accomplishment
Upper level	Self-actualization	Self-fulfilment, personal enrichment

At each level, different priorities exist in terms of the benefits a customer is seeking. The implication is that one must first satisfy basic needs before ascending to higher needs. It is worth mentioning that one product or service may satisfy a number of different needs simultaneously – for example, a meal at a fashionable and expensive restaurant can obviously meet a range of needs, from physiological to ego and self-actualization.

It is probably fair to say that most of the products and services we purchase in modern economic markets have a significant element of the upper-level motives at the root of our perceived needs – for example, clothing (designer clothes and shoes, etc.), motorcars (luxury saloon cars, performance cars, 'super cars', etc.).

Values

Our motives are filtered through our values. Values can be defined as our broad preferences concerning appropriate courses of action or outcomes and they reflect our sense of 'good' and 'bad'. Our values develop in a number of ways but the family (with its socialization of children) is a major factor, along with school, religion and peer group influence.

For example, motives such as prestige and status (ego needs) would be manifested as different perceived needs in individuals with different values. If we take this example further, when considering the purchase of a prestige motorcar, a customer whose values include a heightened awareness of environmental issues is likely to have a different set of perceived needs from a customer who does not share that value and may consider a hybrid vehicle as more attractive.

Attitudes

Over time, we all develop a set of attitudes. Attitudes are a predisposition or a tendency to respond positively or negatively towards a certain stimulus – such as an idea, a person, a situation or a product. Our attitudes incorporate both our motives and our values but they are also influenced by our experiences.

For example, for most of the twentieth century, smoking was prevalent in the UK and often depicted as part of a 'glamorous, film star' lifestyle. However, over time the prevailing attitudes to smoking have changed, mainly due to medical research evidence linking smoking with serious health conditions. Legislation was introduced making enclosed public places smoke-free (in 2006 in Scotland and 2007 in England and Wales), which has further driven attitudinal change. To quote an NHS report from 2009:

> 'Just over two-thirds (69%) [of respondents] said that smoking was not allowed at all in their home in 2008/09, similar to the 67% in 2007 but a statistically significant increase since 2006 when 61% of people said this. A fifth (20%) said it was allowed in some rooms or at some times and only 10% said it was allowed everywhere.'

> (Source: *Opinions Survey Report No. 40, Smoking-related Behaviour and Attitudes,* 2008/09, National Statistics Opinions Survey produced on behalf of the NHS)

This demonstrates the powerful effect changing attitudes can have on people's behaviour and, from the marketing standpoint, their buying behaviour. It also shows the link between societal and political (legislation) influences – part of the PEST environment mentioned earlier (and discussed again in more detail later in the book).

⚇ COACHING SESSION 23

Customer motives

For your product or service, consider the customers who buy your offering.

Which motive/s do you think are being satisfied by them when they purchase your offering? Write them down in the space below.

_____

_____

_____

_____

If you have more than one offering, you will need to conduct this exercise for each offering.

_____

_____

_____

_____

HOW (AND WHY) CUSTOMERS CAN BE 'SEGMENTED'

As we saw in Chapter 1, customers are different. They may differ in terms of their values and attitudes, their incomes, age, gender or location, and these differences are the reason why we seek to segment markets. Segmentation, as we said, refers to dividing customers into segments where customers within one segment have similar characteristics and as a segment are different from customers in other segments.

We can imagine a number of ways in which customers can be organized as market segments:

- Geographical – this can be based on countries, regions within countries, etc.
- Demographic – this can be based on age, gender, family size, income, occupation, education, race, religion, etc.
- Behavioural – this can be based on consumer knowledge, perceptions, attitudes, uses of and responses to a product or service.

Fundamentally, the basis for segmenting a market must be founded on differences in customers' perceived needs. However, in practical terms, it is sometimes difficult to identify – and therefore to direct marketing effort at – potential customers on this basis.

While it is relatively easy to identify customers and potential customers by age or sex or by where they live, such variables do not always correspond to customers' buying preferences. This has led marketers to seek to record customers' preferences through mechanisms such as loyalty programmes (e.g. Nectar). An alternative approach combines a range of data sources to profile customers and create segments based on customers' buying behaviour (e.g. CACI's Acorn, a geodemographic tool used to classify and understand the UK population and its demand for products and services.)

Three other important characteristics are required for effective segmentation. They are that the market must be:

- **measurable** – if we cannot measure the market in terms of market worth (i.e. monetary spend), numbers of customers, etc., it is difficult to develop strategies to exploit these segments
- **accessible** – if we cannot access customers in terms of the media they are exposed to, where they shop, etc., it is again difficult to develop strategies to exploit these segments
- **of sufficient size** – unless the segment has critical mass, it will not be cost-effective for the company to target it.

Interestingly, research ('Have you tested your strategy lately?' *McKinsey Quarterly,* January 2011) suggests that businesses should consider more rather than fewer segments ('...think in terms of 30–50 segments, not 5 or so'). To quote the authors:

'Defining and understanding these segments correctly is one of the most practical things a company can do to improve its strategy.'

Moreover, as we saw in Chapter 1, 80 per cent of variance in revenue growth is explained by choices about *where* to compete (market segments) and only 20 per cent by *how* to compete. Effective segmentation is critical to success and we shall return to this issue later in the book.

COACHING SESSION 24

Your customer segments

Consider the characteristics of all the customer segments your organization currently serves. Don't forget to include the three important characteristics for effective segmentation set out above, i.e. measurable, accessible and of sufficient size.

Write them in a list below.

Segment 1:

_____

_____

_____

Segment 2:

_____

_____

_____

Segment 3:

_____

_____

_____

Segment 4:

_____

_____

_____

HOW CUSTOMERS SELECT FROM DIFFERENT OPTIONS

How customers select from different options is known as 'customer behaviour' and it has traditionally been seen as a problem-solving process. Implicit in this is that customers act in a logical manner when selecting solutions to their needs. As described in Chapter 1, this process is a series of steps:

Problem recognition

↓

Information search

↓

Evaluation of options

↓

Product choice

↓

Outcomes

We can look at each step in turn.

Problem recognition

This would be the point where a customer articulates their 'perceived need'. In reality, customers tend to have a number of perceived needs that are important to them in meeting their overall needs. Such needs tend to have different levels of importance to the individual customer – this is known as the customer's **hierarchy of needs** – a ranked list of those needs that must be satisfied to convince the customer to act (i.e. buy the product or service).

For major purchases like a home or a car, customers may have a long list (generally in their minds but sometimes written down) of perceived needs. Sometimes such lists can run into double figures, but research suggests that, even when there is a relatively long list of perceived needs, the actual purchase decision is often based on the three or four most important perceived needs.

Information search

Information search can involve a wide range of activities, from looking at manufacturers' brochures and advertisements, reviews in magazines or specialist consumer advisory groups (such as *Which?*), to online searches for user blogs. One important source of information is the opinions of personal contacts such as family, friends and colleagues. Such personal contacts are known as 'significant others', which can be anyone with a strong influence on an individual's self-evaluation. Put another way, 'word-of-mouth' is a very important element of both obtaining information and forming an opinion of an offering.

Evaluation of options

Evaluation of options involves the customer in a comparison of the benefits of a number of solutions (i.e. competitive offerings) against their perceived needs. Clearly, an important element of this is that our offering will be compared against the competition. The customer will make a judgement about which offering has the best match of benefits to their needs and this will normally produce a ranking of best match to worst match. Clearly, price may differ from offering to offering.

The customer now has to decide which offering is the best **value**, i.e. has the most benefits at the lowest price. This can be a difficult problem for the customer when both the number of benefits and the price vary from offering to offering.

Product choice

Product choice leads to the act of purchase. At this stage, buyers may experience pre-purchase anxiety, which is when they worry about the ramifications of the act they are about to commit ('Is it the right product for me?', 'Can I afford it?', 'Will my friends like it?' and so on.). In some cases this leads to the customer postponing a purchase. Marketers are obviously keen to minimize the effect of pre-purchase anxiety to ensure that the buying act takes place.

Outcomes

Outcomes can be described as the 'consumption' stage. This is the stage where the customer actually gets to consume the benefits carried by the offering. We can see now that there are two stages when the customer is evaluating the benefits in the product, which are:

- the pre-purchase stage, up to and including the purchase
- the post-purchase stage.

In the post-purchase stage the product must fulfil the promises made at pre-purchase stage. Its failure to do so will mean little likelihood of a repeat purchase. This is an important business imperative – it is costly to 'create' a customer and, if we fail to satisfy them, we will provide an opportunity for our competitors.

HOW THE TWO MAIN MARKETS DIFFER

We have said that organizations can be customers. Generally, it is considered that organizational markets are different from consumer markets in four key ways:

1. Business-to-business (B2B) markets have a relatively small number of customers – for example, there are relatively few motorcar manufacturers in Europe.

2. Demand for products and services is 'derived demand' – derived from the need to meet the objectives of the organization rather than to be consumed for their own sake, as in the case of consumer markets. For example, car manufacturers buy steel sheet not for its own sake but as a part of the process of producing motorcars for consumption by consumers.

3. Decision-making concerned with specifying and procuring products and services is normally a complex interaction of individuals within and sometimes from outside the organization (e.g. consultants), so that, for instance, technical staff will specify and buying professionals will procure.

4. The perceived needs of the organization will involve a complex interaction of the stated corporate needs and the personal needs of the individuals involved in the decision. A company may specify what is required but this will be interpreted by individuals and will therefore be filtered through their own motives, values and attitudes.

WHERE TO OBTAIN INFORMATION ON CUSTOMERS

We can see that identifying customers' needs is an essential element of developing a marketing plan. Understanding customers' motives and buying behaviour is complex, but managers need this information to reduce risk in decision-making. We can obtain this information from marketing research.

We can define marketing research (MR) as follows:

'Marketing research is the function that links the consumer, customer, and public to the marketer through information – information used to identify and define marketing opportunities and problems; generate, refine, and evaluate marketing actions; monitor marketing performance; and improve understanding of marketing as a process. Marketing research specifies the information required to address these issues, designs the method for collecting information, manages and implements the data collection process, analyses the results, and communicates the findings and their implications.'

(Source: American Marketing Association (AMA))

Internal data

The place to start the research process is *within* the organization. Modern information technology (IT) enables organizations to produce a wide range of information including financial and accounting, production/process, etc. From a marketing perspective, businesses also generate a wide range of information concerning the relationship between the organization and its customers. This information might include:

- sales volumes – by product range

- sales trends – tracked over time, seasonality

- sales by segment – type of customer, geographical location

- requests for product information – responses to advertisements, website 'hits'

- complaints – obviously it is important that complaints are dealt with effectively, but complaints also provide a useful source of information: customers who complain may be articulating a view of a larger, silent group of customers

- reports from salespersons – particularly in B2B markets, salespersons' reports are very important in managing the marketing/sales effort.

You will note that there is a strong link here between the business audit and the customer element of the market audit.

Secondary research

Secondary research can be described as research conducted by others, not necessarily focusing on our particular information needs. The four broad sources are:

1. government data – e.g. the Office for National Statistics (www.ons.gov.uk)

2. non-departmental public bodies (NDPB) – e.g. Ofcom (the independent regulator and competition authority for the UK communications industries) http://stakeholders.ofcom.org.uk

3. trade and professional bodies – e.g. the Society of Motor Manufacturers and Traders (www.smmt.co.uk)

4. commercial research organizations – e.g. Mintel (www.mintel.com) and Keynote (www.keynote.co.uk).

Secondary research offers the advantages of relatively low cost (compared with primary research) and it is often instantly available. Moreover, some research (e.g. the Census) would be impossible for one organization to undertake.

However, there are drawbacks. Since secondary research does not necessarily focus on our particular information needs, care must be taken not to 'fit' the needs of the research to the information available. Also, as the research is already available, it may be too old to meet our requirements. We must take care to assess the degree of accuracy of the secondary research – i.e. how was it gathered, analysed and interpreted?

COACH'S TIP

Use your 'privileged insights'

A huge amount of data is available – from within your organization and from a whole range of suppliers in the marketplace, most of which your competitors also see. To have a competitive advantage, your strategy must rest on 'privileged insights', often from your own commissioned research – your primary research.

Primary research

Primary research refers to research designed and conducted to meet specific research needs. Primary research often builds on secondary research, but primary research will engage directly with the defined marketplace.

There are four broad forms of primary research:

1. **Quantitative**

   This uses some form of random sampling and structured data collection (such as a questionnaire). The findings from quantitative research are representative of the population from which the sample is drawn within defined levels of representativeness. The findings can be presented in quantitative form: '65% of respondents think our product is very good.' Many people will be familiar with quantitative research from being asked to participate in a survey or from seeing survey findings or opinion poll results referred to in the media.

2. **Qualitative**

   This focuses more on understanding the underlying motives and drivers for people's actions. Typically, judgement rather than random sampling is used and sample sizes are much smaller. Consequently, the findings cannot be said to be representative in quantitative terms (as in quantitative research). Qualitative research uses tools such as depth interviews and focus groups.

3. **Observation**

   This involves gathering data by observing relevant people, actions and situations. This type of research is selected when researchers cannot obtain the required information through direct questioning. Observation can include using trained observers (to observe customers' behaviour in a supermarket, for example) and machine-based observation (such as electronic counting of footfall into a shopping mall).

4. Experimental

This uses control samples (two or more samples drawn from different populations) to obtain causal information about links between independent variables such as socio-economic group, age or gender and dependent variables such as product preferences.

Using agencies and doing surveys

It is quite feasible for organizations to conduct their own research studies, but managers often choose to use marketing research agencies because of their experience and expertise. In addition, agencies bring emotional detachment to the problem and, by providing extra resources, enable client staff to concentrate on their core objectives. For more information about selecting and commissioning MR agencies, visit www.mrs.org.uk

If you do choose to conduct your own primary research, you can use a multi-client or 'omnibus' survey, so called because clients can join and leave the 'omnibus' according to their needs. The advantages include cost savings (because the sampling and screening costs are shared across multiple clients) and timeliness (because omnibus samples are large and interviewing is ongoing). For an example of an omnibus supplier and further information, visit www.ipsos-mori.com/omnibusservices.aspx

Alternatively, it is possible to set up an online survey using an intermediary such as Survey Monkey. One drawback of this is that, because respondents are choosing to complete your questionnaire, it is possible that those who choose to respond *may* be different from those who choose not to respond. If the non-respondents hold different attitudes and perceptions from those who respond, this could mean that the results we obtain from the returned sample are biased.

CASE STUDY: JD SPORTS (JD)

JD (part of JD Sports Fashion plc) is the UK's leading retailer of fashionable sports and leisurewear. Founded in 1981 in Manchester, JD today is a nationally recognized UK high street fascia. The JD Sports Fashion Group now has over 900 stores across the UK and Europe and a reputation for stocking exclusive and stylish ranges.

Marketing research enables JD to assess more accurately the level of demand for its products. It also influences decisions to target capital investment on projects that will offer the best return on that investment, such as opening a new store or entering a new market. Marketing research provides consumer feedback. It is essential for JD to have this dialogue with the consumer to gain insight into what they think about its range of products, brands and services. This enables the business to meet its demands and outperform the competition. It helps the business develop a clear and informed strategic business plan, which all business colleagues can work towards fulfilling.

JD uses a mix of secondary and primary research.

Examples of secondary research include:

- Government census data – data gathered every ten years across the UK on factors such as population size, ages and occupations in a location.

- Geodemographic data – collected by specialist agencies (such as Acorn from CACI), this segmentation tool profiles consumers based on their life stage (e.g. marital status, number of children) and their lifestyle (e.g. newspapers read, leisure activities, TV programmes watched).

- Commercial market research reports – prepared by research experts such as Mintel, these provide estimates of the size (volume of sales) in each product or market category and market share by operators within these sectors. At JD this information is invaluable when assessing new product markets (e.g. outdoors) or international opportunities (e.g. France and Spain).

Examples of quantitative market research at JD include:

- Exit surveys – carried out face-to-face with consumers as they leave the store. This is a simple survey covering a cross section of stores to gather the views of consumers in different locations and regions. At JD the purpose of the survey is primarily to understand the reasons for visit, frequency of visit/purchase and reasons for and against purchase.

- The 'shopping bag' survey – the JD research team monitors what carrier bags customers entering JD stores are carrying. This helps identify what other stores JD's customers use and are spending money in. It provides competitor insight and an idea of which retailers attract a similar customer profile to JD, a variable that can influence the location of new JD store openings.

- On-site fieldwork – JD's dedicated site research team invests significant time researching new locations. This involves defining the extent of a location's catchment area, reviewing the presence and quality of the competition and assessing the pitch and visibility (i.e. how busy the area is) of a unit. This helps build a detailed SWOT analysis of each new site.

Examples of qualitative research at JD include:

- Focus groups – by speaking at length with small groups of eight to ten people, more insightful questions can be asked regarding brands and new product developments. At JD these are typically run in schools and colleges, where it can get direct feedback from its core consumers.

- Depth interviews – this involves a researcher accompanying the consumer on a shopping trip in store. This drills deeper into shopper behaviour and their reactions to stores.

JD has well-established research mechanisms to provide ongoing feedback. These provide a mix of qualitative and quantitative market data obtained directly from consumers and from published research. By understanding its consumer base, JD has established itself as the market-leading retailer of fashionable sports and leisure wear.

(Source and for the full case study, visit: http://businesscasestudies.co.uk/jd-sports/using-market-research-to-support-decision-making/introduction.html#axzz2WpigvCd4)

! COACH'S TIP

Key tasks for your secondary research

1. Start with a search of the Office for National Statistics website.

2. Search for other sites based on linkages to your information requirements – include non-departmental public bodies, trade and professional bodies, etc.

3. Search for commercial research firms – decide how much you are prepared to pay for commercial research based on your view of the value of the information available.

COACHING SESSION 25

Conducting a customer market audit

There are four stages in conducting a customer market audit. Go through the following stages and answer the questions below.

Stage 1: Internal review

From our in-house records, what do we currently know about our customers?

_____

_____

_____

_____

What can we say are the opportunities and threats we face? Make a list.

_____

_____

_____

_____

Stage 2: Secondary research

What information requirements do you think are important in terms of assessing market opportunities and threats?

_____

_____

_____

_____

_____

What can we say are the opportunities and threats we face? Make a list.

_____

_____

_____

_____

Stage 3: Primary research

What are your key 'need-to-know' information requirements?

_____

_____

_____

_____

How are you going to obtain this information? Will you commission a research agency, use an omnibus, or conduct the study yourself (perhaps using an intermediary such as Survey Monkey)?

_____

_____

_____

_____

Stage 4: Consolidation

What are the key opportunities and threats that you have identified from the stages above? Make your consolidated list here.

_____

_____

_____

_____

_____

_____

→ NEXT STEPS

In this chapter we have:

- moved our focus to the first part of the market audit – in particular, the opportunities and threats presented by customers and potential customers

- seen that customers' perceived needs are based on motives and customers' values and that attitudes can have a marked effect on their perceived needs

- considered the importance of market segmentation and looked at the key characteristics of effective segmentation

- looked at customer behaviour and the stages involved in making a purchase

- looked at where we can obtain information on customers to help us in the marketing planning process and the stages to be undertaken to capture that information.

The next chapter will focus on the opportunities and threats posed by competitors. It will provide approaches to how to analyse and evaluate competitors including assessing their recent 'track record', i.e. business performance through ratio analysis, their declared corporate objectives/strategies and their customers' (within segments) perceptions of their offerings.

👍 TAKEAWAYS

What thoughts have you had about your customers' perceived needs being based on motives? How do your customers' values and attitudes affect their perceived needs for your products or services?

_____

_____

_____

_____

_____

_____

_____

_____

_____

Now that you have considered the importance of market segmentation, are you taking into account the key characteristics of effective segmentation for your market?

_____

_____

_____

_____

_____

_____

_____

_____

_____

_____

Have you ensured that each of your segments can be measured, is accessible, and is of an appropriate mass to make it cost-effective to target?

_____

_____

_____

_____

_____

_____

_____

_____

_____

_____

_____

Looking at customer behaviour and the stages involved in making a purchase, will you now be able to obtain the information you need on customers to help with the marketing planning process?

_____

_____

_____

_____

_____

_____

_____

_____

_____

_____

_____

Were you able to complete Coaching session 25 as a result of reading this chapter? If not, how could you obtain the information you need to do so?

_____

_____

_____

_____

_____

_____

_____

_____

THE MARKET AUDIT: COMPETITORS

✔ OUTCOMES FROM THIS CHAPTER

- Understand the importance of competitor analysis.
- Know how to define competitors.
- Analyse your competitors – their performance, objectives, strategies, strengths and weaknesses.

THE IMPORTANCE OF COMPETITOR ANALYSIS

Just about every marketplace you can imagine has an element of competition in it. This might be competition from:

- direct competitors
- new entrants
- substitute offerings.

Understanding our competitors is key to developing an effective strategy and therefore core to developing our marketing plan. In Chapter 2 we defined strategy as 'a plan for successful action based on the rationality and interdependence of the moves of opposing or competing participants'.

As in a game or a sport, we improve our chances of winning if we understand our opponent's strengths and weaknesses and if we can use that knowledge to our advantage. For example, if you play tennis, it is good to know such things as whether your opponent has a strong serve, which areas of the court they favour to serve to, and whether they have a strong or weak backhand. Even if we are an inferior player, we can improve our chances of success by not playing to our opponent's strengths while seeking to exploit their weaknesses.

COACH'S TIP

Improve your chances of winning

To improve your chances of winning over your competitors, you need to have a clear picture of their strengths and weaknesses so that you can develop different strategies to defend against their strengths and exploit their weaknesses. Even weaker players can win surprisingly often when deploying a divergent strategy. See *How the weak win wars, A theory of asymmetrical conflict*, Ivan Arreguin-Toft (Cambridge University Press, 2005).

To be able to develop a strategy, we have to *understand* our competitors. In my experience, managers tend to have a poor understanding of their competitors and this has a damaging effect on strategy development. This poor understanding is often born out of being too close to the subject: 'We compete with them every day, so we know all about them.' To counter this problem, we need to adopt a more rigorous approach to analysing our competitors. Clearly, those organizations that systematically and regulalrly profile their competitors have a significant competitive advantage.

DEFINING OUR COMPETITORS

Our first task is to define our competitors. As we have said, competition can come from:

- direct competitors – those currently targeting the same customer segments as we are

- new entrants – those not currently targeting our customer segments but likely to do so in the future

- substitute offerings – new or different ways to satisfy the same needs of our target customer segments as our offerings.

Direct competitors

Let's start by asking ourselves who are our direct competitors. You could simply write down a list of who you think your competitors are, but first consider the following approach to defining competitors:

> 'Our direct competitors are any organizations or individuals that our target customers consider at the second and third stages of the selection process.'

These are the 'information' and 'evaluation of options' stages of the customer behaviour model we looked at in Chapter 5. This is fundamental – it is our customers and potential customers who dictate who we are competing with. It follows that, if we are active in more than one market segment, it is possible that we may encounter the same and/or different competitors as we move from segment to segment.

COACHING SESSION 26

Naming your competitors

Go back to Coaching session 24, where you set out the characteristics of the customer segments your organization currently serves.

Write down against each segment the names of those organizations or individuals you currently understand to be your competitors in these segments.

Segment 1:

_____

_____

_____

_____

Segment 2:

_____

_____

_____

_____

Segment 3:

_____

_____

_____

_____

Segment 4:

_____

_____

_____

_____

New entrants

One could argue that new entrants are less of a threat to us than current competitors and, up to a point, that is a reasonable conclusion. However, the increasing rates of change we have witnessed in the business environment demonstrate that new entrants can become major competitors in a very short time. For example, the following bar chart shows the Internet share in percentage terms of the average weekly value of all retailing in the UK in the period 2006–11.

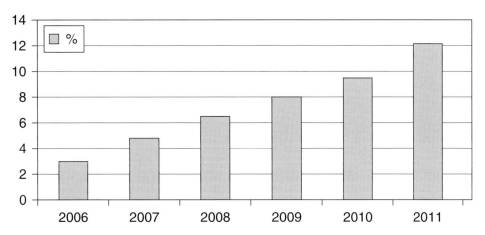

Internet share (%) of average weekly value for all retailing in UK month of November for each year

(Source: _Retail Sales – November 2011_, Office for National Statistics, UK)

These data show the significant growth (up from 3 per cent in 2006 to 12.2 per cent in 2011) in market share obtained by Internet-based retailing in the UK.

It is necessary, therefore, that we monitor those organizations that have the 'capability' to be considered by our target customer segments at the 'information' and 'evaluation of options' stages of the customer behaviour model.

This means identifying organizations that:

- could enter our sector (perhaps through new technology), particularly where they can offer similar levels of product benefits at a cheaper price (the way Amazon.com entered the retail market in a number of countries)

- have a synergy with our sector but are not currently active in it (the way Porsche moved into the luxury four-door saloon performance-car segment by launching the Panamera model to compete with BMW, Mercedes, Audi and Jaguar)

- currently supply us but could develop their capability (by acquisition, for instance) to compete directly with us (the way the oil companies such as BP and Shell have their own retail outlets in the form of branded petrol stations)

- are currently our customers but could set up in competition with us (by acquiring one of our competitors, for instance) through reverse vertical integration (the way that Lafarge Tarmac is a leading UK construction materials and services joint venture company as well as the UK's market leader in the supply of aggregates).

COACHING SESSION 27

New entrants to your marketplace

Consider those organizations that you think are the most likely new entrants to your marketplaces.

Write down their names and how they could do this below.

1 _____

2 _____

3 _____

4 _____

5 _____

6 _____

Substitute offerings

Even where an organization is seen to have a dominant market position, there are substitute offerings that can compete for its customers. For instance, around half of all diamonds originate from central and southern Africa and De Beers is the leading business in this marketplace. However, cubic zirconia and moissanite are seen by some customer segments as viable substitutes for diamonds.

Identifying substitute offerings is a matter of searching the 'environment' for offerings that can perform the same function as our offering. Quite often, these new or different ways of meeting customer needs are technology driven. For instance, the LP (long player) record was substituted by the music CD, which in turn was substituted by digital downloads and, in the first three months of 2012, UK digital music revenue exceeded sales of physical formats such as CDs and records for the first time (source: British Phonographic Industry).

COACHING SESSION 28

Potential substitutes to your offering

Think about the potential substitutes to your offering that are most likely to present a competitive threat in the near future. Consider technological change as part of this.

Write down your list below.

1 _____

2 _____

3 _____

4 _____

5 _____

6 _____

ANALYSING OUR COMPETITORS

The four main areas of competitor analysis are:

1. performance
2. objectives
3. strategies
4. strengths and weaknesses.

We shall look at the processes involved for each.

Performance

As we saw in the business audit in Chapter 4, we can learn much about the strengths and weaknesses of an organization by looking at their performance. The most obvious place to start is with their turnover and profitability performance.

Limited companies include these performance data in their annual reports. Quoted companies (those quoted on the London Stock Exchange or on NASDAQ) produce annual reports that are submitted to Companies House in the UK (www.companieshouse.gov.uk/) or EDGAR in the US (www.sec.gov/edgar. shtml) and often included as a download on their websites. Also, you can contact an organization's Company Secretary and request a copy of their annual report.

The London Stock Exchange (LSE) website provides a useful analysis page for each quoted company, covering performance data for the last five years. Search by company name and look for 'fundamentals':

www.londonstockexchange.com/home/homepage.htm

In addition, LSE offers a free 'company profile' service:

www.londonstockexchange.com/prices-and-markets/stocks/tools-and-services/company-profile/about-profile/about-profile.htm

The NASDAQ Stock Market offers a similar service in the US: www.nasdaq.com

There are around 26 stock exchanges in the USA (plus electronic exchanges). For more information, see:

www.world-stock-exchanges.net/usa.html

One problem is identifying data at a product or sector level. Often, large businesses aggregate their results and this can make 'unbundling' their detailed performance difficult. One tip is to look at the 'Notes to financial statements', normally at the back of the report. In this section you can sometimes find breakdowns of turnover and profit by segment.

All limited companies must file an annual report and in the UK Companies House provides a service (called Web Check) that allows you to order copies of company documents online for a small fee per document:

wck2.companieshouse.gov.uk//wcframe?name=accessCompanyInfo

A particular problem with smaller companies is that they can withhold their turnover and profit figures by adopting the abbreviated form of accounts, in accordance with Section 226 of the Companies Act 1985. In this case it is possible to estimate turnover from their debtors figures, based on an assumption of how long debtors take to pay. For instance, the following debtors figures were taken from a set of company accounts submitted to Companies House and retrieved via Web Check.

We can estimate the sales figures from the reported debtor figures by assuming that this company provides 60 days' credit to its debtors:

	Current year	Previous year
Debtors £000s	652.3	911.5
Estimated sales £000s	3,968	5,545

*Debtors divided by 60 days multiplied by 365 days

A number of commercial organizations also provide information on companies, including:

- Dun & Bradstreet (D&B) – www.dnb.com/ or www.dnb.co.uk/
- Keynote – www.keynote.co.uk/business-intelligence/ratio-reports

Alternatively, Marketresearch can be interrogated at a product and country level:

www.marketresearch.com/

Partnerships and sole traders do not have to declare their figures, so it is much more difficult to obtain detailed turnover and profit data for them. However, it is sometimes possible to obtain information from other sources, such as their websites, promotional material and information provided to the press for publication (i.e. press releases). One approach is to cross-reference sources and look for corroboration.

Charities have to submit their financial reports to the Charity Commission. Profiles of charities are presented on the Commission's website:

www.charitycommission.gov.uk/find-charities/

Once we have obtained competitor performance data, we must analyse it. It is worth looking back at Chapter 4, to the section headed 'A review of recent performance' to see how we analysed in-house data. The following example uses similar ratios to analyse competitor performance. These data are also drawn from real businesses, but with some changes to protect identities.

The five companies shown in the table below are direct competitors in a one-service marketplace; these five businesses represent the total market for this service. The performance figures have been drawn from company accounts filed with Companies House and accessed via Web Check. For information, the measure of profit is **operating profit,** which is the profit earned from a firm's normal core business operations. This value does not include any profit earned from investments – such as earnings from firms in which the company has partial interest – and the effects of interest and taxes.

The following table presents summary performance data for the client company and its four competitors (Competitors A to D), along with ratio analysis to highlight performance strengths and weaknesses.

Summary performance data & ratio analysis – client and four competitors

Most recent year		Client company	Competitor A	Competitor B	Competitor C	Competitor D
Turnover (TO)	£ m	87.9	84.4	40.5	52.3	180.5
Operating profit (OP)	£ m	1.5	4	2.7	0.69	10.9
OP to TO	%	1.7	4.7	6.7	1.3	6.0
Number of employees	No.	650	741	613	636	2,795
TO to employees	£000s	135.2	113.9	66.1	82.2	64.6
Capital employed (CE)	£ m	3.6	10.3	7.8	11.2	32
Return on CE	%	41.7	38.8	34.6	6.2	34.1
Previous year						
Turnover (TO)	£ m	94.5	94	44.3	77.9	179.9
Operating profit (OP)	£ m	3.5	2.3	2.6	0.5	10.2
OP to TO	%	3.7	2.4	5.9	0.6	5.7
Number of employees	No.	635	735	611	823	2,788
TO to employees	£000s	148.8	127.9	72.5	94.7	64.5
Capital employed (CE)	£ m	4.4	11.3	7.8	10.9	38
Return on CE	%	79.5	20.4	33.3	4.6	26.8

COACHING SESSION 29

Comparing competitor data

Using the information presented in the table above, answer the following questions.

In the most recent year, which business was the market leader?

Client   A   B   C   D

In the most recent year, which business had the best operating profit to turnover performance?

Client   A   B   C   D

In the most recent year, which business had the best productivity (i.e. turnover to number of employees)?

Client   A   B   C   D

In the most recent year, which business had the worst return on capital employed?

Client   A   B   C   D

Which business had the biggest fall in turnover most current year on previous year?

Client   A   B   C   D

(See Appendix 3 for the answers.)

Objectives

Understanding our competitors' objectives allows us to gauge whether they are likely to change their strategy in the future. For instance, in our example above, Competitor C showed the biggest fall in turnover in the most recent year compared to the previous year. If we know that the stated objective of Competitor C is to become market leader, then we could expect it to make significant changes to the way it competes in the future.

In addition, knowing what our competitors' objectives are will give us some clues to how they might respond to a new threat, such as a new entrant or a substitute offering.

Our competitors' objectives are likely to develop in the same way as ours. You will remember from Chapter 3 that corporate objectives often develop from a series of qualitative objectives (such as a mission statement) and are translated into quantitative business objectives to allow ongoing measurement of performance.

Gathering information about competitors' objectives needs a subtle approach, often drawing on a wide range of sources to produce a picture of their underlying objectives. Some of the best sources are:

- annual reports, Chairman's and Chief Executive's statements
- announcements to investors (including annual general meeting of shareholders)
- press cuttings from business press, general press and specialist industry publications (e.g. *Construction News*)
- company websites
- company promotional materials (including hard copy and videos)
- senior executives' attendance as speakers at conferences and seminars
- company's social networking presence (e.g. Facebook and Twitter)
- following key staff on LinkedIn
- customer newsletters
- employee newsletters.

Strategies

The difference between objectives and strategy is that strategy is the way we plan to achieve our objectives. However, by definition, objectives and strategy must be closely related.

In his book *Competitive Strategy*, Michael Porter developed the concept of the 'three generic strategies'. This says that the strategies of all companies can be classified into one (or sometimes more) of three generic strategies.

Porter's three generic strategies are presented in the following model:

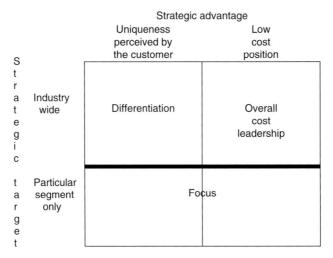

The three generic strategies

(Source: Michael E. Porter, *Competitive Strategy* (Free Press,1998))

The three generic strategies can be summarized as follows:

1. **Overall cost leadership**

   Here, managerial emphasis is on cost minimization and control. This strategy provides the business with a defence against rivals because it can still earn returns after its competitors have competed away their profits through rivalry.

2. **Differentiation**

   Here, management seeks to differentiate the product or service by creating something that is perceived industry wide to be unique – e.g. brand, technological advantages, patents or control of scarce resources.

3. **Focus**

   Here, management focuses on a specific buyer group and seeks to serve that target particularly well, either through uniqueness perceived by the customer or low-cost position.

Porter also says that the three generic strategies are viable approaches to dealing with competitive forces. However, a business failing to develop its strategy in at least one of the three directions – a 'stuck-in-the-middle' firm – is in an extremely poor strategic situation and is almost guaranteed low profitability.

Consequently, we can use Porter's three generic strategies to classify the strategic approaches of our competitors. Gathering information about competitors' strategies uses the same sources as those set out for understanding their objectives. One important additional source of information is customer perception, considered in the next section.

Strengths and weaknesses

We can look at our competitors' strengths and weaknesses in two ways:

- in terms of customers' perceptions
- in terms of our analysis of them at a functional level – their marketing, operations, human resources and finance.

As we have seen, the perceptions of our customers and potential customers dictate whom we are competing with. Therefore it is important that we understand the perceptions of our customers in terms of their views of our strengths and weaknesses and the strengths and weaknesses of our competitors.

Clearly, if we are going to use this understanding in a practical way, we need information. The process involved in obtaining this information is primary research (see Chapter 4), normally a mix of:

- **qualitative research** (such as focus groups) to understand customers' perceived needs and the relative importance of each perceived need and also to isolate the competitors they would consider at the 'information' and 'evaluation of options' stages of the customer behaviour model
- **quantitative research** to capture customers' perceptions of our product and our competitors' products in terms of the match to customers' perceived needs.

This analysis provides us with a powerful picture of the customers' perceptions of both our strengths and weaknesses and those of our competitors. We will look at the mechanics of this process in more detail in Chapter 8.

The second way of looking at our competitors' strengths and weaknesses is through our analysis of them at a functional level – their marketing, operations, human resources and finance.

- **Marketing**

    We can review our competitors' marketing strengths and weaknesses by using the same marketing mix checklist we considered in Chapter 4, when we conducted the business audit of our own organization.

- **Operations**

    Operations are the things that organizations do to deliver satisfied customers and meet organizational objectives. Clearly, a review of a competitor's operations depends on the nature of its offering. For instance, a review of the operational strengths and weaknesses of TNT and Aldi would emphasize very different factors because of the different nature of these businesses.

■ **Human resources**

People are, some argue, the most important asset for any organization, and people, through their actions, create satisfied customers. Assessing the strengths and weaknesses of the HR function of competitors involves drawing on a range of areas – from review of senior management (experience and background), current size and make-up of the workforce, recruitment policies and recruitment goals (which may indicate what the competitor is planning), to training and development policies.

! COACH'S TIP

Where to find information about competitors

You can obtain much of the information you need from published sources such as annual reports, press releases and company websites. In addition, it is always worth speaking with recent ex-employees of competitors, who can give an insider's view of their strengths and weaknesses.

■ **Finance**

As well as analysing competitors' published accounts, we could produce a broader analysis that could include liquidity (the current ratio we defined in Chapter 4), capital and reserves (which give an indication of overall financial strength and funds available for expansion), to assess the financial strengths and weaknesses of our competitors.

⌕⌕ COACHING SESSION 30

Conducting a customer market audit

Using the list of competitors you prepared in Coaching session 26, work through the four main areas of competitor analysis. You will need to do this for each competitor you encounter in your target segment/s, so be prepared to spend a considerable amount of time on this.

Performance

1 _____

2 _____

3 _____

4 _____

5 _____

Objectives

1 _____

2 _____

3 _____

4 _____

5 _____

Strategies

1 _____

2 _____

3 _____

4 _____

5 _____

Strengths and weaknesses

1 _____

2 _____

3 _____

4 _____

5 _____

ONLINE RESOURCE

Comparing client to competitors table

For a copy of the table, go to:

www.TYCoachbooks.com/Marketingplanning

NEXT STEPS

In this chapter we have:

- seen that we can improve our chances of winning if we understand our opponent's strengths and weaknesses – the main reason for conducting competitor analysis as part of a market audit

- categorized competitors as direct competitors (those currently targeting the same customer segments as you), new entrants (those not currently targeting your customer segments but likely to do so in the future) and substitute offerings (new or different ways to satisfy the same needs of our target customer segments as our offerings)

- considered the four main areas of competitor analysis – performance, objectives, strategies, and strengths and weaknesses.

In the next chapter we are going to focus on the third and final part of the market audit, the PEST analysis, and look at how we can draw together all the stages of our audit to produce a consolidated market audit. In addition, we will look at establishing information gathering and analysis as part of the management information system within the organization.

TAKEAWAYS

As a result of reading this chapter, do you understand the importance of competitor analysis? What can you usefully incorporate into your ideas about marketing planning?

_____

_____

_____

_____

_____

_____

_____

_____

Have you been able to define your competitors under the three main categories – as direct competitors, new entrants and substitute offerings? What has this shown you about the competition for your organization?

_____

_____

_____

_____

_____

_____

_____

_____

_____

_____

When considering the four main areas of competitor analysis – performance, objectives, strategies, and strengths and weaknesses – how do you think your findings from this will inform your marketing plan?

_____

_____

_____

_____

_____

_____

_____

_____

_____

If you have seen that there are gaps in your marketing planning, what do you plan to do to address them?

_____

_____

_____

_____

_____

_____

_____

_____

_____

_____

_____

_____

THE MARKET AUDIT: THE MARKETPLACE

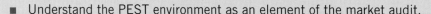

OUTCOMES FROM THIS CHAPTER

- Understand the PEST environment as an element of the market audit.
- Recognize the significance of the PEST audit in the marketing planning process.
- Know how to conduct a PEST audit.
- Know how to set up a marketing information system (MkIS).

WHAT IS THE PEST ENVIRONMENT?

The final step of our focus on the analysis stage of the marketing planning process is to look at the PEST 'environment' and its effect on the marketplace, to gain an overview of the opportunities and threats it might pose.

We examined the idea of an organization existing in a business 'environment' in Chapter 4, when we introduced the idea of PEST as part of a SWOT analysis. PEST refers to four forces that impact on both the organization and the other players in the marketplace, including customers, potential customers, competitors and suppliers. These forces are:

- **P** – political
- **E** – economic
- **S** – society or societal
- **T** – technological.

We can consider some examples of these forces at work.

Political

In essence, this refers to the impact that government has on the marketplace, both directly and indirectly. Governments pass laws and regulations and make policies that can have significant effects on a marketplace, and these effects may be defined as either opportunities or threats.

Legislation For instance, in Chapter 5 we referred to the UK legislation making enclosed public places smoke free (The Health Act 2006). This legislation posed a threat to the tobacco companies: research by Nielsen in the UK in July 2007 showed that cigarette sales in England fell by 11 per cent compared with a year earlier. Other research (Health Behaviour Research Unit, University College London) has pointed to a significant reduction in the numbers of smokers, likely to produce opportunities for other products like aids to give up smoking and e-cigarettes.

Another important example of UK legislation is the Climate Change Act 2008. The Act makes it the duty of the Government to ensure that the net UK carbon account (for all six Kyoto greenhouse gases) for the year 2050 is at least 80 per cent lower than the 1990 baseline. The Act aims to enable the UK to become a low-carbon economy and gives ministers powers to introduce the measures necessary to achieve this aim. This legislation thus poses a major threat to industries involved in fossil-fuel-based activities but also provides opportunites for businesses engaged in new technologies.

To quote the CBI:

> 'The UK's energy infrastructure needs £200 billion in investment over 20 years. That means this must be the decade of delivery. Tackling climate change means using energy more efficently, future-proofing businesses against climate threats and moving business operations towards carbon neutrality. Only by enabling the market to develop the solutions we need will we achieve these goals.'

(Source: www.cbi.org.uk/business-issues/energy-and-climate-change)

Other factors Other political factors that can create opportunities and threats include tax policies (for individuals and businesses), trade restrictions and tariffs, and control of certain goods and services (such as banned substances).

In addition, the Government is a major 'customer' to many industries. For instance:

- the construction and civil engineering industries obtain a significant share of their turnover from the Government (e.g. road and rail infrastructure projects)
- in the UK the NHS is the main customer for the pharmaceutical industry
- education departments of local government are a major source of business for organizations serving the education sector.

Economic

The macro-economic situation has an important bearing on opportunities and threats. For instance, the Bank of England sets the base rate (i.e. the interest rate at which they lend money to other financial institutions such as banks and building societies). One of the Bank of England's two core purposes is monetary stability – stable prices, low inflation and confidence in the currency. Stable prices are defined by the Government's inflation target, which the Bank seeks to meet through the decisions taken by the Monetary Policy Committee.

Clearly, lowering or raising interest rates affects a wide range of business sectors both directly and indirectly. For example, house building can be directly affected – home buyers can be deterred from taking on a mortgage when interest rates go up – but this can also have an indirect effect – home owners with mortgages will have less money to spend on other goods and services if interest rates go up and their monthly mortgage payments increase. Similarly, increasing levels of unemployment due to poor economic growth can significantly reduce levels of demand in the economy.

Reducing the amount of disposable income in the economy can create both opportunities and threats. For example, for the restaurant and hospitality sector a reduction in disposable income would be a threat, whereas the major supermarkets would see it as an opportunity to develop 'meal deals' for customers to 'dine out at home'.

Society or societal

Societal factors can include changes in attitudes and values, such as attitudes and behavioural changes regarding smoking at home, mentioned in Chapter 5, and more structural changes to the population like an increase in the proportion of the population in the older age groups. The latter, often referred to as 'demographic' factors, can produce a wide range of opportunities and threats. For instance, an ageing population may provide a market for a different range of products and services than younger people.

Technological

This aspect of the PEST environment includes all those developments that come from science and technology and influence how we live our lives and the kinds of products and services that we see as relevant to our perceived needs. Looking at the products and services available today compared with 20 years ago, we can see that many technological developments have dramatically changed the way we live our lives. From the proliferation of Internet access to the development of mobile communications technology, these technologies have provided a platform for a wide range of new products and services.

CASE STUDY: LOGICA

Logica is an innovative IT services organization that brings people, business and technologies together. Logica employs more than 41,000 people and has clients around the world in a variety of industries, including automotive, oil and gas, and manufacturing. Logica's services aim to add value for clients through, for example, improving efficiency and productivity or reducing waste. The work of Logica is not just about developing technology. It is about getting business benefits from the technology available. It is also about enabling clients to reduce environmental impacts. Logica's experts increasingly provide sustainable and long-term solutions for its customers.

Here are some examples of the PEST factors affecting Logica:

Political factors

Public sector budget cuts by the UK government and increased university fees are affecting the education sector. These changes in the educational landscape could have an impact on the number of potential employees with the skills and competencies that Logica requires.

Economic factors

The global economic recession has affected how most firms conduct business. As businesses focus on areas where efficiencies can be made, some might choose to outsource functions to reduce costs, rather than employing people with specialist skills. This has created increased demand for outsourced services such as those Logica offers. Logica's employees have the specialist IT skills required to offer businesses of all types efficient and effective ways to manage systems and processes.

Social factors

The UK has an older and more diverse society with people from many different backgrounds and cultures. A diverse workforce brings together people with different skills and competencies. Diversity is therefore a focus of Logica's HR strategy. Logica competes with many other firms for a limited pool of highly talented individuals with good IT and numerical skills. To increase this pool of talent, Logica aims to increase the number of females in its workforce. Within the IT industry, women account for an average of only 16 per cent of the graduates in Computer Science/IT.

Technological factors

The speed of technological advances means that existing electronic equipment, IT processes and systems will quickly become dated. To remain competitive, a business must ensure that its processes and systems support innovation and creativity for itself and its customers. Logica has embraced recent advances in technology to offer its clients the most advanced and sustainable services possible. An example of this is the use of 'cloud' technology. Cloud technology allows companies to access and buy into data storage or software 'on demand' through the Internet.

By monitoring and auditing its own external environment, Logica has also been able to adapt its business to maximize efficiency and exploit opportunities. This has been done through adjusting its service offering to utilize advancements in technology and drive improvements to IT services for clients.

(Source and for the full case study visit:

www.businesscasestudies.co.uk/logica/using-skills-to-respond-to-the-external-environment/introduction.html#axzz2XVbmC5gL)

This case study illustrates how PEST factors can impact on a company's strengths and weaknesses and ultimately on their competitive advantage:

1. This is a clear example of how an economic factor can create an opportunity – the recession has created a pressure on businesses to outsource their IT activities and this offers Logica a business opportunity.

2. The political decision to increase university tuition fees may have an adverse effect on the number of suitably qualified people available for recruitment by Logica in the future. Given that a highly trained and qualified staff is a central strength for Logica, the business had to respond to this threat. Consequently, Logica developed in-house training (Level 3 Apprenticeship) and launched its own sponsored BA (Hons) degree programmes (Business Management and Business Management with IT).

CONDUCTING A PEST AUDIT

It can be quite a daunting task to embark on a PEST analysis for the first time. Given that there are potentially so many different factors that could have an impact on your organization, how do you focus on those that are most important? The best place to start is with your products and services and the markets you serve. You can use the PEST headings to scan the business environment for factors likely to have an influence on your planning.

This PEST topic is very broad and generally it is better to focus on sources most closely linked to your product and/or service. For some specific sources of information, see Appendix 4.

 COACH'S TIP

Focus on what's relevant

Remember that your focus should be on the factors likely to have an impact on your marketing planning period (most likely the next three years). Guard against being drawn into 'blue sky thinking' that lacks relevance to the development of your plan.

COACHING SESSION 31

Conducting a PEST review of your marketplace

To conduct a PEST review of your marketplace, you will need to assemble a resource base for each of the four environmental factors – political, economic, societal and technological – and then list the opportunities and threats you perceive in the environment.

Summarize your analysis in the table below.

	Opportunities	Threats
Political		
Economic		
Societal		
Technological		

SETTING UP A MARKETING INFORMATION SYSTEM

The tasks you have carried out in this and the preceding two chapters constitute a significant body of work, but you can use this work as the basis for setting up an in-house, ongoing information source, or marketing information system. A formal marketing information system (MkIS) can be defined as:

> 'a system in which marketing data is formally gathered, stored, analysed and distributed to managers in accordance with their informational needs on a regular basis'.

The MkIS process involves four stages:

1. **Information requirements**

   An MkIS starts with a definition of the information requirements, i.e. the information required by managers to help them reduce risk in decision-making.

2. **Data sources**

   MkIS will draw on a wide range of information, both from within the business (i.e. as we've suggested above) and from other sources outside the business. External sources are likely to include:

   - marketing intelligence
   - secondary research (including competitor and PEST analysis)
   - primary research (qualitative and quantitative).

3. **Data processing** (to generate information)

   There is a difference between data and information. Data are the raw facts, which may not necessarily be related to helping management reduce risk in decision-making. Modern IT systems can generate significant volumes of data that can threaten to engulf managers. Information, on the other hand, is knowledge relevant to a specific requirement.

COACH'S TIP

Collect the right information

The critical focus for the MkIS is that it must produce information *appropriate* to the decision needs of the users.

4. Dissemination of information

For the information to be of value, it must be disseminated to those who can obtain value from it. It is important, therefore, that the output of the MkIS is designed to meet the needs of the users, i.e. it is relevant, easily understood, clear and concise.

NEXT STEPS

In this chapter you have:

- looked at the PEST 'environment' and considered how opportunities and threats can derive from these PEST forces

- looked at a range of sources of information on PEST factors, including official, government and commercial sources

- acknowledged that this kind of analysis (and the other stages of the market audit) demands a significant amount of effort

- learned how to set up a marketing information system to capture, analyse and disseminate such information in the future.

The next chapter will look at how we can produce a consolidated SWOT analysis based on the strengths and weaknesses identified in the business audit along with the opportunities and threats identified in the market audit. We will then go on to strategically 'position' the organization – i.e. to decide which segments the organization will choose to focus on.

TAKEAWAYS

Having looked at the PEST (political, economic, societal and technological) 'environment', have you considered some examples for your own organization of how opportunities and threats can derive from these PEST forces?

_____

_____

_____

_____

_____

_____

_____

_____

_____

_____

What sources of information on PEST factors – including official sources (such as the Government) and other sources including those which provide information on a commercial basis – do you think will be most useful to you, and why?

_____

_____

_____

_____

_____

_____

_____

_____

_____

_____

_____

Have you worked out how much time you think you will need to carry out the kind of analysis described in this chapter? When and how will you set aside this time?

_____

_____

_____

_____

_____

_____

_____

_____

_____

_____

A marketing information system is a useful way to capture, analyse and disseminate such information in the future. What are the challenges for you in setting one up?

_____

_____

_____

_____

_____

_____

_____

_____

_____

_____

8

SWOT ANALYSIS AND STRATEGIC POSITIONING

OUTCOMES FROM THIS CHAPTER

- Draw together the findings from the business audit and the market audit.
- Produce a SWOT analysis consolidating your findings.
- Understand the process of strategic 'positioning' to decide which segments the organization will select to focus on.
- Look at a worked example of strategic positioning.

PRODUCING A CONSOLIDATED SWOT ANALYSIS

The findings from the business audit and the market audit will provide a sound basis for commencing the strategic positioning exercise. However, we have seen that it is likely that these two exercises will produce a relatively large body of data. Clearly, to make this information digestible and useful for us, we need to produce a consolidated SWOT (strengths and weaknesses and opportunities and threats) analysis. To do this, we need to:

- assemble the raw SWOT data by source (see Chapters 4–7: in-house records, customers, competitors, PEST)
- process these data in terms of assessing the strengths and weaknesses and opportunities and threats that each produces
- assess the relative importance of each in terms of meeting the organization's objectives; this is a relatively subjective exercise and one approach is to use a weighting system (see below)
- produce the consolidated SWOT presenting each factor ranked in terms of its relative importance.

COACH'S TIP

Keep it concise

The consolidated SWOT, ideally, should be no longer than four pages of A4 (roughly one page per element).

COACHING SESSION 32

Producing your SWOT analysis

Using the approach described above, produce your own consolidated SWOT analysis.

Fill in the table below.

Strengths	Weight*

Weaknesses	Weight*

Opportunities	Weight*

Threats	Weight*

*Weight relative importance scale of 1–10, where 10 is critical

THE PROCESS OF STRATEGIC 'POSITIONING'

The strategic positioning or targeting exercise is the heart of the marketing planning process. Decisions made at this stage will have a significant effect on the overall success of the plan. The strategic positioning process we are going to use is based on **decision theory** and its practical counterpart, **decision analysis**.

The basic issue is that, when human beings seek to optimize their performance, they often make poor selection choices when faced with many alternative courses of action. This problem is compounded when we move to a 'committee' situation where we have a number of decision-makers working in concert, because different individuals can have very different perceptions of what the objectives are and the relevant merits of various courses of action.

We have already emphasized the benefits of involving a number of individuals in the marketing planning process and setting up a marketing planning team. This means we need a framework that both helps us control for ambiguity (and therefore differences in perceptions) and provides the basis for reducing complex issues relating to alternative courses of action to a more simplified format.

The purpose of the strategic positioning exercise is to match the organization's strengths to opportunities in the marketplace, so that the firm can obtain the best return on effort. The marketing planning team therefore has two distinct tasks:

1. Rank the market segments in terms of their attractiveness to the organization.

2. Rank the organization against the competition in terms of attractiveness to the market segments.

These two tasks can be represented in the following matrix.

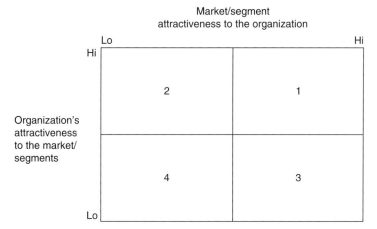

The strategic positioning or targeting matrix

Let us consider each cell in turn:

- **Cell 1** represents segment/s that are highly attractive to the organization and the organization is highly attractive to the buyers in the segment/s. This is the most effective matching of the organization to the segment/s.

- **Cell 2** is where the organization is still highly attractive to the segment/s but the segment/s are less attractive to the organization (e.g. the segment/s may be too small or offer poor creditworthiness). In this case, we may choose to 'sub-segment' these segments to isolate the most attractive segments that may be worthy of targeting.

- **Cell 3** represents segments attractive to the organization but that do not perceive the organization to be attractive to them. In this case, we need to assess the basis of this perception. If our offering is objectively poorer than our competition, then we must do something to address this disadvantage (e.g. improve product quality). However, if we can find no objective difference between our offering and that of our competitors, the problem is one of perception and we may be able to move this favourable perception in our direction (i.e. through our communication strategy).

- **Cell 4** is where both the segment/s is/are unattractive to the organization and the organization is unattractive to the segment/s. We would want to 'de-target' (i.e. redirect resources *away* from) these segments in such circumstances.

Stage 1: Rank the attractiveness of market segments to the organization

The steps in the process are as follows:

1. Define and list the markets/segments to be reviewed.

2. When considering the relative attractiveness of different segments, list up to ten criteria important to the firm. These criteria might include issues of risk and profitability, and also be related to segment size and segment growth.

3. Apply weightings to each criterion in terms of its importance to the firm. Use a 10-point scale, where 10 is the most essential and 0 is the least essential.

4. Consider each segment against each criterion and score (S) this in terms of how good or poor the segment is, where 10 is the highest score and 0 the lowest.

5. Multiply the criteria weights by the segment scores to produce a **weighted score** (WS).

6. Sum the weighted scores for each segment under review.

7. Convert the total weighted scores to percentages (TWS %) where 100% = the total weights × 10.

Stage 2: Rank the attractiveness of the organization to the market segments

This second stage is the 'other side of the coin' and the steps are as follows:

1. For each segment under review, list the hierarchy of needs – those perceived needs that determine which supplier a customer within that segment would favour.

2. Apply weightings to each identified need in the hierarchy of needs in terms of its importance to the customers in the defined segment. Use a 10-point scale where 10 is essential.

3. Identify and list those competitors that the firm will face in this defined segment. Focus only on the key competitors.

4. Consider the firm and each competitor against each perceived need, and score (S) this in terms of how good or poor the firm/competitors are, where 10 is the highest score and 0 the lowest.

5. Multiply the perceived needs weights by the firm/competitor scores to produce a **weighted score** (WS).

6. Sum the weighted scores for the firm and each competitor under review.

7. Convert the total weighted scores to percentages (TWS %) where 100% = the total weights × 10.

Conduct these two stages of the exercise for each segment under review.

 COACH'S TIP

Make your matrix easy for everyone to read

It is advisable to use a relatively large blank matrix to make it 'easy on the eye'.

A WORKED EXAMPLE OF STRATEGIC POSITIONING

We can return to our example of ABC Ltd, first considered in Chapter 4. The table below sets out the process for scoring and producing weighted scores for three market segments that have been selected by the marketing planning team for ABC Ltd – these are Segment A, Segment B and Segment C.

ABC's marketing planning team would have defined the market segments under review by using the information gathered through the SWOT analysis.

The next step is to define our criteria of importance – the issues that are important to the firm when considering the relative attractiveness of different segments. Again, earlier work such as our business audit and the establishment of our strategic and marketing objectives will provide the basis for this stage.

Since we must guard against ambiguity, we may need to have fuller descriptions of what we mean when describing our criteria. For instance, the criterion 'profitability' in the table below is somewhat vague in this format, so it would need to have a fuller description, such as 'Profitability: to deliver contribution levels better than 12.5% of sales revenue'.

 COACH'S TIP

Guard against ambiguity

To benefit from this process, we must make sure that all members of the marketing planning team have a clear understanding of both the definitions of the segments under review and the criteria we are applying to assess their attractiveness to us.

The next step is to score each segment in terms of how good or poor it is, relevant to the defined criterion. This stage involves not just reliance on objective information already gathered as part of the SWOT analysis but also the knowledge and experience of the members of the marketing planning team. For example, 'Sales volumes' is likely to refer to the overall market size and therefore the potential market share available to ABC Ltd. In this situation, secondary research (part of the market audit) can provide useful objective information. In practice, this stage uses a focus group format to consider each segment and to negotiate a team score.

Market/segment attractiveness

Criteria	Weight	Segment A Score	Segment A WS	Segment B Score	Segment B WS	Segment C Score	Segment C WS
Good credit risk	6.6	6.6	43.6	8.3	54.8	7.9	52.1
Profitability	9.6	5.4	51.8	6.2	59.5	5.9	56.6
Sales volumes	8.3	9.5	78.9	8.8	73.0	8.7	72.2
Segment size	7.5	7.3	54.8	4.3	32.3	6.1	45.8
Channel selection	5.9	4.6	27.1	5.2	30.7	8.6	50.7
Total WS	37.9		256.1		250.3		277.5
TWS %			67.6		66.0		73.2
Max. possible score =	379						

ABC's marketing planning team have given Segment C the highest weighted score of 73 per cent, followed by Segment A and Segment B, on 68 and 66 per cent respectively. This makes Segment C our primary target segment.

ABC's marketing planning team now needs to focus on ranking the organization against the competition in terms of attractiveness to the customers in these segments. Given that Segment C is the most attractive segment to us at this stage, let's look at our relative attractiveness to the customers in Segment C.

The starting point is to list the hierarchy of needs (i.e. those perceived needs that determine which supplier a customer within that segment would favour). The most effective way to obtain this information is through primary marketing research. Careful drafting of the question structure and content can enable us to obtain information in the direct format we require. For instance, we could obtain the initial hierarchy of needs from qualitative research (such as focus groups) and then use this list to conduct quantitative research to uncover the relative importance of each perceived need by using a 1–10 scale, where 10 is most essential and 0 is least essential.

The next step is to list those competitors we believe we will encounter in Segment C. Again, primary research with customers from Segment C will help us develop this list, but business audit information and management knowledge will also help.

The next step is to establish how well or poorly the customers in Segment C perceive the firm and each competitor on the listed hierarchy of needs. Fundamentally, primary research should be the basis for this.

The firm's and competitors' attractiveness to customers in Segment C

Hierarchy of needs	Weight	Firm score	Firm WS	Comp. 1 score	Comp. 1 WS	Comp. 2 score	Comp. 2 WS	Comp. 3 score	Comp. 3 WS
Reputation (brand)	7	6	42.0	7	49.0	6	42.0	5	35.0
Reliability/ quality	6	8	48.0	4	24.0	2	12.0	5	30.0
Customer service	8	4	32.0	9	72.0	2	16.0	6	48.0
Availability	5	9	45.0	4	20.0	4	20.0	5	25.0
Location	3	9	27.0	2	6.0	7	21.0	7	21.0
Total WS	29		194.0		171.0		111.0		159.0
TWS %			66.9		59.0		38.3		54.8
Max possible score =	290								

The table shows that the customers in Segment C perceive the firm, ABC Ltd, to be the best match of benefits to their hierarchy of needs. ABC Ltd is nearly 8 percentage points above its nearest rival, Competitor 1, and 12 percentage points above the next rival, Competitor 3. We might consider Competitor 2 to be not really a serious competitor for ABC Ltd in this market segment.

We can plot the relative positions of the firm and its three competitors on the matrix we introduced earlier. (For convenience, the firm's attractiveness to the market/segments is referred to as 'competence'.)

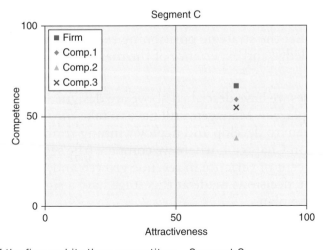

Relative positions of the firm and its three competitors – Segment C

The analysis in the previous table and the pictorial representation in the matrix above provide us with an interesting format for considering our strategic moves and those of our competitors.

As we have said, ABC Ltd (the firm) is perceived by the customers in Segment C to be the best match of benefits to their hierarchy of needs. However, if we look closely at the scoring, Competitor 1 significantly out-scores ABC Ltd on the most important perceived need: customer service. This perceived need has the highest weight (8) and Competitor 1 scores 9 against ABC's score of 4. Clearly, the management of ABC Ltd must take note of the competitive threat posed by Competitor 1. For instance, if the management of Competitor 1 could double their score for reliability/quality from 4 to 8, they would overtake ABC Ltd as the supplier perceived by customers in Segment C to be the best match of benefits to their hierarchy of needs.

Probably the best strategic response from ABC would be to focus on the need with the highest score – customer service – and improve customers' perceptions of their performance on this need. If ABC were to improve its perceived performance on customer service from 4 to 8, its overall score would increase from 66.9 to 77.9 per cent.

This worked example is relatively simplistic – we only considered three segments, and we have only conducted the positioning analysis on one segment. In addition, our analysis of this segment is based on only four 'players': the firm and three competitors. In reality, you are likely to face more segments and more competitors. However, the process and value inherent in the analysis would be the same, regardless of the numbers of segments or competitors under review.

Another important point worth making is that much of the second stage (the firm's and competitors' attractiveness to customers) is based on primary research with customers from the defined segments. Gathering such information naturally takes time and has a cost. However, such information has significant value in reducing risk in decision-making and is strongly recommended. Where there is simply no time (or resource) available to obtain such primary research data, you can conduct the strategic positioning exercise using secondary research data and the knowledge and experience of the members of the marketing planning team.

Finally, the processes we have described above are designed to aid decision-making – not to replace it. Managers still have to take the information and insights and use them to develop and deploy winning strategies. As we saw from research presented in Chapter 1, where we compete (the segments we target) will account for 80 per cent of variance in revenue growth and, as we stated at the start of this chapter, decisions made at this stage have a significant effect on the overall success of the plan.

COACHING SESSION 33

Strategic positioning exercise

Use the Excel templates you downloaded from the website to complete your positioning exercise.

Step one: ranking the market segments in terms of their attractiveness to the organization
1. Define and list the markets/segments to be reviewed.
2. List those criteria that are important to the firm when considering the relative attractiveness of different segments.
3. Apply weightings to each criterion in terms of its importance to the firm. Use a 10-point scale, where 10 is essential.
4. Consider each segment against each criterion and score (S) this in terms of how good (i.e. a high score, 10 being the highest) or poor (i.e. a low score, 0 being the lowest) the segment is.
5. Multiply the criteria weights by the segment scores to produce a weighted acore (WS).
6. Sum the weighted scores for each segment under review.
7. Covert the total weighted scores (TWS %) to percentages where 100% = the total weights x 10.

Step two: ranking the organization against the competition in terms of attractiveness to the market segments
1. For each segment under review, list the hierarchy of needs (i.e. those perceived needs that determine which supplier a customer within that segment would favour)
2. Apply weightings to each identified need in the hierarchy of needs in terms of its importance to the customers in the defined segment. Use a 10-point scale, where 10 is essential.
3. Identify and list those competitors that the firm will face in this defined segment.
4. Consider the firm and each competitor against each perceived need and score (S) this in terms of how good (i.e. a high score, 10 being the highest) or poor (i.e. a low score, 0 being the lowest) the firm/competitors are.
5. Multiply the perceived needs weights by the firm/competitor scores to produce a weighted score (WS).
6. Sum the weighted scores for the firm and each competitor under review.
7. Convert the total weighted scores (TWS %) to percentages where 100% = the total weights x 10.
8. Conduct this exercise for each segment under review.

Step three: placing each segment on the matrix
1. Add the criteria of attractiveness score to the horizontal.
2. Add the firm's attractiveness (or competence) score to the vertical.

Using % scores (TWS %) means that you can use a standardized matrix (i.e. maximum 100, minimum 0) and allows direct comparisons between different segments and different competitors.

COACHING SESSION 34

Selecting your target segments

Using the analysis you developed in Coaching session 33, think about your strategic moves and those of your competitors. You may want to consider the following questions:

1. Which segments are most attractive to us?

_____

_____

2. Which segments perceive us to be most attractive to them?

_____

_____

3. How close are our competitors to us in these segments?

_____

_____

4. What are our competitors' scores on the most important perceived needs in these segments?

_____

_____

5. What might our competitors do to improve their scoring and what can we do to maintain our leadership position?

_____

_____

6. On the basis of the above, select and list your target segments.

_____

_____

_____

_____

_____

_____

ONLINE RESOURCE

Segment C matrix

Download the matrix from this website:

www.TYCoachbooks.com/Marketingplanning

→ NEXT STEPS

In this chapter we have:

- set out a method for producing a consolidated SWOT analysis from the business audit and market audit work reviewed in Chapters 4–7

- discussed the nature and importance of a strategic positioning or targeting exercise

- set out a process for conducting a strategic positioning exercise

- worked through an example of a strategic positioning exercise to illustrate the processes involved.

The next chapter will focus on the marketing mix and show that it involves deciding what to produce, how much to charge, where the customer will buy the product and how to inform and persuade the customer to buy the product. In addition, you will learn about the procedures for defining a product strategy – how to ensure that the product or service delivers benefits matched to customers' perceived needs.

TAKEAWAYS

What are the key things you have learned from this chapter about producing a consolidated SWOT analysis?

_____

_____

_____

_____

_____

_____

_____

_____

_____

_____

Having gone through the process of conducting a strategic positioning exercise, what did you find challenging about it and why?

_____

_____

_____

_____

_____

_____

_____

_____

_____

_____

_____

What one thing will you do differently in the future as a result of reading this chapter?

_____

_____

_____

_____

_____

_____

_____

_____

_____

9

THE MARKETING MIX: PRODUCT

 OUTCOMES FROM THIS CHAPTER

- Recognize the link between the marketing mix and the strategic positioning exercise.
- Understand the function of the product strategy.
- Distinguish between product features and benefits.
- Understand the stages of the product life cycle and the need for new product development.
- Know how to make product strategy decisions.

DEVELOPING THE MARKETING STRATEGY

Now that we have completed the strategic positioning exercise in the previous chapter, we are ready to focus on developing the marketing strategy. As we have seen in Chapter 1, there are four components of the marketing mix or marketing strategy: product, price, place and promotion. Put another way, they are: deciding what to produce; how much to charge; where the customer will buy the product; and how to inform and persuade the customer to buy the product. This chapter looks in detail at the first element of the marketing mix, product.

Chapter 3 introduced the idea of the marketing planning process as a flow chart, in which the strategic positioning or targeting exercise came immediately before the (development of the) marketing strategy or marketing mix. Through the process of the strategic positioning exercise, we have identified and isolated the segments that offer the best match of our strengths to the perceived needs of the customers in these target segments, so that our organization can increase the probability of achieving its stated objectives.

Each of the target segments we have chosen presents opportunities to create effective marketing strategies. In this and the next three chapters we are going to look in detail at the work needed to create marketing strategies to exploit these target segments.

Developing the marketing strategy or marketing mix needs to focus on how we are going to:

- meet the needs of the customers in our target segments
- integrate our marketing activities – our product, price, place and promotional activities – for maximum effect.

Integration of our marketing activities is central to meeting our marketing objectives. The use of the term 'mix' accurately depicts what we need to do – i.e. we need to *mix* together the four elements of the marketing strategy (the four Ps) to produce a coherent and cohesive strategy to meet our objectives. It is critical that the 'mixing' is effective not only from the customers' standpoint but also from an internal organizational efficiency standpoint. For instance, the TNT case study in Chapter 1, shows that the firm was taking considerable steps to develop their customer focus strategy and, to support the communication of this, they developed their 'customer promise', which provided them with a platform for their promotional strategy.

THE FUNCTION OF THE PRODUCT STRATEGY

As we have seen, a product – whether it is very tangible such as a car or very intangible such as a haircut – carries benefits that satisfy customers' needs. The product is the fundamental basis of the relationship between the organization and its customers. In the context of the marketing mix, we can define 'product' as 'anything offered to the marketplace that can satisfy a customer's perceived need'.

Products need to be *matched* to the target segments they are aimed at. That means ensuring that the product can deliver what the customers need. It therefore follows that, if an organization has more than one target market segment, they are likely to need a range of products to meet the needs of all the customer segments they are targeting. Consequently, the starting point is the *hierarchy of needs* for the customers in the defined segment. The product targeted at this segment must contain benefits aligned with customers' hierarchy of needs – i.e. the needs at the top of their list that are the most important to them – and our product must match benefits to this list.

Since a product can be tangible or intangible, it is possible to establish a tangible–intangible continuum, with highly tangible products at one extreme, (e.g. salt) and highly intangible products at the other extreme (e.g. insurance):

The tangible–intangible continuum

You can place any product or service on the above continuum based on the tangible/intangible mix. Let's look at some examples.

- Motorcars

  The physical nature of the product has a high element of tangibility, but there are intangible benefits such as the brand, dealer service, etc.

- Personal computers

  This has a high element of physical product, but brand and pre- and post-service support add intangible benefits.

- Restaurants

  The food is tangible but the overall benefit is made up of intangibles such as the decor, the ambience, the service and the restaurant's reputation (and hence its status).

- Perfumes

  The core offering is intangible in terms of the benefits customers derive from the purchase but the offering is 'delivered' as a tangible product. Interestingly, part of this tangibility includes the packaging.

The importance of brand

A very important form of intangible benefit is the brand. A brand is:

> 'a name, term, sign, symbol, association, trademark or design which is intended to identify the products or services of one provider or group of providers, and to differentiate them from those of competitors. A brand has functional and emotional elements that create a relationship between customers and the product or service'.

Customers develop loyalty to a brand based on previous experience, i.e. they have purchased the product before and found that it has met their perceived needs. Alternatively, a brand can be associated with a lifestyle or particular condition that is important to the customer and that they aspire to.

In addition, brands can add value to a product. For instance, fashion brands such as Armani, Dolce & Gabbana, Gucci and Versace offer intangible benefits to the customer in terms of meeting important needs such as self-actualization and the esteem of others (see Maslow's hierarchy of needs described in Chapter 5).

Branding helps buyers identify products that might benefit them and tells them something about product quality and consistency. In frequent purchase situations it can also help customers save time.

Brand management seeks to make the product or service relevant to the target segments. Brands should be seen as more than the difference between the actual cost of a product and its selling price; brands represent the sum of all valuable qualities of a product to the customer. Branding is therefore a function of successful relationships with customers.

PRODUCT FEATURES AND BENEFITS

There is an important difference between product features and product benefits. A product, whether predominantly tangible or intangible, must carry benefits that satisfy customers' needs. Benefits are those elements of the product that meet customers' needs. Features, on the other hand, carry those benefits.

In marketing, then, it is important to differentiate between a benefit and a feature. Telling customers about a feature may not enable them to understand how the product will meet their perceived needs. Features are the product's capabilities; benefits are the outcomes customers 'consume' by way of meeting their perceived needs.

For example, many motorcars today have antilock braking systems (ABS) as standard. ABS is not a benefit per se but a feature that carries a benefit, as shown in this table.

Feature	Benefit	Need
ABS	Safer breaking	Safety

Customers don't care about features unless they're experienced in buying the specific type of product we are offering. Many potential customers will be put off by what they consider 'jargon' because they cannot see what benefits these features would offer to them.

In essence, they ask, 'What's in it for me?' In this case, what does the ABS feature provide that is of benefit to me? People with an understanding of what ABS means can make a judgement about the benefits of ABS in a motor vehicle offering, based on a list of features. In effect, the features list can be shorthand between the experienced customer and the producer.

THE PRODUCT LIFE CYCLE

Most products display similar characteristics to living organisms, in that they are 'born', grow to maturity, decline and 'die'. In this way, products display a 'life cycle', known as the product life cycle (PLC).

While the life expectancy of products varies greatly, most products go through four stages: introduction (1), growth (2), maturity (3) and decline (4), as shown graphically below.

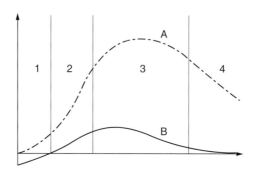

The product life cycle

The horizontal axis of the graph represents time and the vertical axis represents sales (depicted by graph line A) and profit (depicted by graph line B). We can consider some of the properties of the four stages.

1. **Introduction**

   At this stage the product has been introduced to the market. Sales growth is slow and profits are negative due to the costs of launch. A group of buyers is adopting the new product. These buyers are known as 'innovators' and they are characterized by their desire for new experiences and a relatively high degree of risk-taking. A rule of thumb says that this group accounts for around 10 per cent of the market.

2. **Growth**

   If the product is perceived to have benefits matched to customers' needs, it will become more widely adopted. Sales will grow quickly and profits will follow suit. The growth stage is driven by a group of buyers known as 'early adopters', who are also characterized by an appetite for new (and better) solutions to their needs but who lack the risk-taking of the innovators. A rule of thumb says this group accounts for around 20 per cent of the market.

3. **Maturity**

   At some point, the product's sales growth will slow and it will enter its mature stage. The maturity stage is commonly the longest period, during which sales and profits peak. The mature stage is characterized by the adoption of the product by the majority of the market, known as the 'late adopters'. This group accounts for around 60 per cent of the market.

4. **Decline**

   At some stage the product's sales are likely to decline. This can be due to new products being seen as a better match to customers' needs, changing customer attitudes, or increased competition. Even during this stage, though, new customers are adopting the product. These customers are known as 'laggards' – people characterized by a generally conservative outlook and a low acceptance of risk. This group accounts for around 10 per cent of the market.

CASE STUDY: THE TYPEWRITER

A good example of the PLC in practice is the typewriter, invented in the 1860s. Typewriters quickly became indispensable tools for practically all writing other than personal correspondence. For the next 120 years they were widely used by professional writers, in offices, and for business correspondence in private homes. Then word processors and personal computers came on the market and, by the end of the 1980s, they had largely displaced typewriters for most of these uses in the developed world. However, as recently as July 2013, Russia's agency responsible for Kremlin security (FSO) placed an order for electric typewriters on the state procurement website, a move reportedly prompted by recent leaks from WikiLeaks and Edward Snowden.

THE NEED FOR NEW PRODUCTS

The key reason why products decline is change. Customers change and the PEST factors change and influence customers, and consequently we must be alert to the need for new solutions to customers' needs. **New product development** (NPD) is therefore an important element of an organization's product strategy.

New products cost an organization until they reach growth stage and some products never achieve this stage and fail, with the resultant impact on the organization's profitability. We have to maximize the chances of a new product becoming established (i.e. reaching the maturity stage of the PLC). NPD success is linked to the **diffusion of innovation**, which is the way new ideas or products are communicated through certain channels over time to a marketplace. Several factors determine whether and how quickly an innovation will be adopted.

- **Relative advantage**

  Potential adopters must perceive that the innovation is an improvement over the previous solution to their needs. In some NPD situations, the customer has a poorly defined need because up to that point there had been no solution to their needs. This is the 'anticipation' element of our definition of marketing.

- **Compatibility**

  Potential adopters must perceive the innovation as consistent with their existing values, past experiences and needs. An idea that is incompatible with their values and norms will not be adopted at all or not as rapidly as an innovation that is compatible.

- **Relative complexity/simplicity**

  If the innovation is too difficult to understand or use, it is less likely to be adopted.

- **Trialability**

  If the potential adopter may try or experiment with the innovation, this will increase the chances of it being adopted.

- **Observability**

  The more easily an innovation is visible to others, the more this will drive communication among peers and personal networks and will in turn create more positive or negative reactions (i.e. the effect of 'innovators' on 'early adopters').

 COACH'S TIP

Focus on needs, not product

Organizations must focus on customers' needs, *not* their product range, if they are to avoid losing customers to better ways of meeting their needs. This was Theodore Levitt's fundamental point in 'Marketing myopia', his famous article published in the *Harvard Business Review* in 1960 (see Chapter 2 of this book).

MAKING PRODUCT STRATEGY DECISIONS

We have to make a series of decisions regarding the product offering. We can summarize these decisions under four headings in the following checklist:

1. **Core benefit** – as we have seen, the product must carry benefits to meet the customers' perceived needs. In general terms we need to:

    i. understand the hierarchy of needs (the relative importance of customers' perceived needs)

    ii. ensure that the product carries benefits– both tangible and intangible – matched to these needs.

2. **Actual product** – in effect, this is the manifestation of the core benefits decisions and this area includes:

    i. product design

    ii. styling

    iii. quality

    iv. colours

    v. branding

   vi. packaging.

3. **Augmented product** – decisions in this area involve anything that can add value to the customer (and differentiate our offering from that of the competition) and could include:

    i. installation

   ii. warranty

  iii. credit facilities

   iv. after-sales service.

4. **Product range depth and width** – decisions in this area involve:

    i. the 'width' of the product range, e.g. small family hatchback, family saloon car, executive saloon car

   ii. the 'depth', i.e. range of engines on offer, trim levels, equipment levels.

An organization may have a number of products, all at different stages of the PLC. This means that we have to take into consideration how we manage the 'portfolio of products'. This means completing the following exercise for each product in the organization's range.

COACHING SESSION 35

Your product strategy decisions

You can now use the product strategy decisions checklist above to set out your own product strategy.

Under the headings below, set out for each of your target segments what your product strategy must contain to meet your objectives.

Target segment 1

Core benefit

_____

_____

_____

Actual product

_____

_____

_____

Augmented product

_____

_____

_____

Product range depth and width

_____

_____

_____

Target segment 2

Core benefit

_____

_____

_____

Actual product

_____

_____

_____

Augmented product

_____

_____

_____

Product range depth and width

_____

_____

_____

Target segment 3

Core benefit

_____

_____

_____

Actual product

_____

_____

_____

Augmented product

_____

_____

_____

Product range depth and width

_____

_____

_____

Target segment 4

Core benefit

_____

_____

_____

Actual product

_____

_____

_____

Augmented product

_____

_____

_____

Product range depth and width

_____

_____

_____

Once you have completed this list, you can ensure that your decisions are translated into actions by completing an action checklist (see Chapter 13).

 **NEXT STEPS**

In this chapter we have:

- looked at the relationship between the strategic positioning exercise and the development of the marketing mix or strategy

- established that we will need a separate marketing mix for each of our target segments

- learned that the product strategy must carry benefits that satisfy customers' needs, which makes it the fundamental basis of the relationship between the organization and the customer

- considered the nature of tangible and intangible benefits and looked at the value of creating brands

- established how product features are different from benefits and identified the need to focus on benefits rather than features

- explored the idea of product life cycles and the need for new product development within the organization

- listed product strategy decision areas to include in marketing planning.

The following chapter will focus on the next stage of the marketing mix – price. Clearly, price is inextricably linked to product strategy because customers make judgements about value based on the benefits in the product matched to their needs and the price of the product. We will explore this relationship and set out how to produce a pricing strategy to meet organizational objectives.

TAKEAWAYS

What have you learned from this chapter about the relationship between the strategic positioning exercise and the marketing mix or strategy?

_____

_____

_____

_____

_____

_____

_____

_____

In what ways will you develop your product strategy to make it the fundamental basis of the relationship between the organization and the customer?

_____

_____

_____

_____

_____

_____

_____

_____

_____

_____

Having gone through the process of conducting a strategic positioning exercise, what did you find challenging about it and why?

_____

_____

_____

_____

_____

_____

_____

_____

_____

_____

What one thing will you do differently in the future as a result of reading this chapter?

_____

_____

_____

_____

_____

_____

_____

_____

_____

_____

_____

10

THE MARKETING MIX: PRICE

✔ OUTCOMES FROM THIS CHAPTER

- Understand the concept of the pricing 'triangle'.
- Recognize the strategic relationship between price and benefits.
- Know how to make pricing strategy decisions.

THE PRICING 'TRIANGLE'

At its simplest, price is the amount a customer must pay to obtain the benefits from a product or service. It is the 'exchange' part of the four 'big ideas' in marketing, discussed in the introduction to this book. However, in practice, there are three interrelated forces acting on any organization's decisions regarding pricing. These are:

- the target audience's perception of value in our and the competition's offerings
- our cost structure
- the competition's price levels.

We can represent this interrelationship as the pricing 'triangle':

The pricing 'triangle'

These three interrelated forces have a major influence on an organization's decisions regarding their pricing strategy. We can look in more detail at each in turn.

Perception of value in offerings

Value is the customer's perception of the match of benefits in an offering to their needs. It is measured by the customer's willingness to pay for it. We can illustrate this with a simple example: a customer sees three products (A, B and C) as having *exactly* the same benefits matched to his or her needs. However, the products have different prices:

Product	Price
Product A	225.00
Product B	264.00
Product C	210.00

In this situation, the product with the lowest price (Product C) offers the best value – i.e. the same benefits as products A and B but at the lowest cost.

However, if each of the three products is perceived to have a *different* bundle of benefits, it is much more difficult for the customer to assess the value in each product. As we have seen, benefits can be tangible and intangible and products can carry a bundle of benefits relevant to a range of customers' needs.

Consequently, the more sophisticated and/or complicated the product and the more variability there is in price levels, the more difficult it is for customers to make a judgement about the value in each and to choose between different products. Customers adopt a range of strategies to deal with this situation. Some customers are very thorough in their analysis of the benefits offered by the competing products and calculate the best value on this basis. Other types of customer will focus on just one or two of their most important perceived needs and make their value judgement on that basis. Others will rely on their experiences of particular brands to guide their decision. Another group will always choose the lowest price option, regardless of the benefits on offer.

Consumer durables (such as cars and washing machines) and many products purchased by organizations have a further value component of **cost over time** – the cost of using the product as well as the cost of acquiring it. In the case of cars it can include fuel economy, road tax band, cost of tyres and cost of servicing. Customers must make a judgement on the relative value of a product based on their expectations of what it will cost to use.

Price can be inextricably linked to the customers' perception of quality and hence value. A product can be 'too cheap' – it is difficult for the customer to accept that the benefits they perceive in the product can be obtained for such a 'low' price. This phenomenon is known as 'customer dissonance' and further illustrates the link between product and pricing strategies.

Our cost structure

Price is not the same as cost. Price is ultimately controlled by customers' value perceptions; cost is the monetary value of producing and delivering the product, including profit. It can be a mistake to simply calculate the cost of a product and add a percentage to cover profit – such an approach may well result in a price that is not aligned with the benefits customers perceive in the product. We need to define costs.

There are two broad groups of costs:

■ **Variable costs** – so called because they vary directly with the level of production – the more we produce, the more variable costs we incur. Examples are raw materials, labour directly linked to production, and operating expenses directly related to production.

■ **Fixed costs** – also known as overheads, these do *not* vary with the level of production. Whether we make anything or not, we will still incur these costs. Examples are office/factory rent, business rates, and salaries of labour not directly involved in production such as administrative and sales staff, and management.

Break-even point

It follows that variable costs are built on the fixed costs to give us our total costs. At a certain level of units of production (and hence revenue), the total cost (fixed and variable) matches the revenue value. This is known as the **break-even point**: as production increases from this point, the organization will make profits.

Break-even point is illustrated in the following graph. The vertical axis represents monetary value and the horizontal axis represents numbers of units (or output).

■ Line 'A' shows the income or revenue line – the more units we sell, the higher the total monetary value will be.

■ Line 'B' represents the fixed cost element of our costs. As you can see, this does *not* vary with output.

■ Line 'C', however, does vary with output and is the variable cost.

To obtain total costs, we need to start the variable cost line at point B on the vertical axis, i.e. where our fixed cost line is. 'P' is the break-even point – the point where the total cost line bisects the income or revenue line (Q is the number of units of output). After the break-even point has been passed (i.e. to the right of it), the business starts to make a profit and, as output increases, so profit increases.

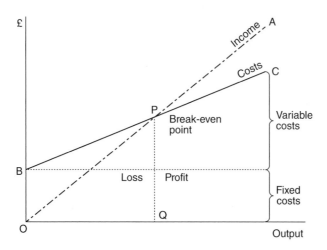

Break-even point

This analysis demonstrates that understanding our fixed and variable costs and knowing where our break-even point is provides us with a clear picture of when we start to become profitable. One interesting point – if we set our price *below* variable cost, we will never make a contribution to our fixed costs or ever make a profit.

The competition's price levels

This is the third point of our pricing 'triangle'. Competitors, like us, will be focusing on understanding customers' needs, matching their benefits to these needs and trying to give the customer the best value proposition. We have seen that, where products offer broadly the same benefits, it is reasonably easy for customers to decide which offers the best value – i.e. the cheapest. Consequently, competitors may try to complicate things by seeking to remove some benefits to reduce price and then offering these benefits as optional extras. Anyone who has bought a motor vehicle will be familiar with this approach.

In many organizations, pricing offers the most immediate and flexible tool in the marketing mix because it is relatively easy to change prices. Consequently, many organizations rely on price cuts to generate sales or to meet a competitive threat. This may be a 'double-edged sword': while a price cut may generate sales in the short term, it may undermine the customers' perceptions of the value they perceive in the product.

Time is an additional variable we need to consider. The product life cycle (PLC) we looked at earlier demonstrates the link between units purchased (revenue) and time. When a new product is launched, some organizations choose to set a high price – this is called **market-skimming pricing**. As the product moves into the mature stage, prices can be reduced to stimulate increased adoption – this is known as **market-penetration pricing**.

COACH'S TIP

Stay vigilant about what customers and competitors are doing

We must remain vigilant and aware of not only what our competitors are doing but, equally importantly (if not more so), what customers are thinking and doing with regard to our offering and that of the competition. It is vital to understand the importance of marketing information, including marketing research, discussed previously.

THE STRATEGIC RELATIONSHIP BETWEEN PRICE AND BENEFITS

We have seen that there is a strong link between the product element of the marketing mix and the pricing element, because of customers' perceptions of value.

When we combine benefits and price, we are faced with four broad relationships, as illustrated in the benefits/price matrix below.

BENEFITS

		Fewer	More
P R I C E	Lower	1	2
	Higher	3	4

The benefits/price matrix

Each cell of the matrix represents a different relationship between our customers' perceptions of our benefits and those of our competitors (fewer, or more) and our price compared with our competitors' prices (lower, or higher). We can explore the implications of each relationship (i.e. each cell) in turn.

- **Cell 4**

    We have a higher price and more perceived benefits than the competition. Does this mean that we win? It depends on the customers' perception of the value of our additional benefits compared with our higher price, i.e. are the extra benefits worth the higher price?

- **Cell 3**

  Our price is higher than the competition's, but we have fewer perceived benefits. Under this scenario, we will lose. We have three choices:

  - reduce the price to make our product better value

  - increase benefits but keep the price the same to improve value

  - 'disinvest' in this market (i.e. stop targeting resources at this market).

- **Cell 2**

  We have more benefits and a lower price than the competition, so we should win. But we are sacrificing profit with our lower price. We may want to do this to create a competitive barrier, which means that competitors may withdraw if they can't see an opportunity to take profitable market share. However, such a situation is not good for our organization's sustainability over the medium to long term.

- **Cell 1**

  We have fewer benefits than the competition but the lowest price. This is the mirror image of Cell 4, and our success depends on the customers' perception of the value we deliver from a lower price compared with the reduced benefits in our offering. This strategy often wins because customers are concentrating on price rather than value.

PRICING STRATEGY DECISIONS

Pricing decisions must take into account the three forces described in the pricing 'triangle' above. However, as we have already said, price is a part of the overall marketing mix and is interrelated with the other parts of the mix. If we operate in an undifferentiated market (e.g. petrol retailing), our pricing strategy will reflect the fact that it is very difficult to differentiate our offering from that of the competition in terms of additional benefits matched to customers' needs. On the other hand, if we operate in the luxury goods market (e.g. fragrances, fine jewellery and watches), we can expect to be able to use our benefits (including intangibles such as brand) to differentiate our offering from that of the competition.

In addition, if we use channels of distribution (which we shall look at in the next chapter), our prices will need to reflect the fact that our intermediaries need to make a margin.

We can summarize our pricing strategy decisions under three headings in the following checklist.

1. **Customers' perceptions** – we must understand the customers' perception of the value in our offering. This means:
    i.   understanding customers' views of the benefits in our product relevant to their needs
    ii. understanding customers' perceptions of the value they obtain from our product based on the *actual* price they pay (which may not be the official or 'list' price and to understand customers' perceptions of value we must know the actual price they pay).

2. **Competitors' offerings** – we must know about the benefits and prices (real) of our competitors' offerings. This involves:
    i.   understanding customers' views of the benefits in our competitors' product relevant to their needs
    ii. understanding customers' perceptions of the value they obtain from our competitors' products based on the *actual* price they pay.

3. **Our cost structure** – we need to know what it costs us to make and provide our product. This involves:
    i.   clear and accurate statements of variable costs
    ii. clear and accurate statements of fixed costs
    iii. estimates of different fixed cost levels at different volumes of production
    iv. knowing our position in the benefits/price matrix compared with our competitors.

COACHING SESSION 36

Your pricing strategy decisions

You can now use the pricing strategy decisions checklist above to set out your own pricing strategy.

Under the headings below, set out for each of your target segments what your pricing strategy must contain to meet your objectives.

Target segment 1

Customers' perceptions

_____

_____

_____

Competitors' offerings

_____

_____

_____

Our cost structure

_____

_____

_____

Target segment 2

Customers' perceptions

_____

_____

_____

Competitors' offerings

_____

_____

_____

Our cost structure

_____

_____

_____

Target segment 3

Customers' perceptions

_____

_____

_____

Competitors' offerings

_____

_____

_____

Our cost structure

_____

_____

_____

Target segment 4

Customers' perceptions

_____

_____

_____

Competitors' offerings

_____

_____

_____

Our cost structure

_____

_____

_____

Once you have completed this list, you can ensure that your decisions are translated into an action checklist (see Chapter 13).

→ NEXT STEPS

In this chapter we have:

- considered the important link between benefits and price
- focused on the three forces that affect pricing decisions
- considered the strategic relationship between price and benefits
- set out a checklist for guiding your pricing decisions.

The next chapter will focus on the next stage of the marketing mix – place. This is where we make decisions that focus on how to make our offering available to customers. We will look at the issues regarding whether intermediaries are needed and, if so, what type. In addition, we will introduce methods to assess the 'added value' an intermediary brings to the marketing mix.

👍 TAKEAWAYS

In what ways will you develop your pricing strategy to take into account the three forces that affect pricing decisions?

_____

_____

_____

_____

_____

_____

_____

_____

_____

What have you learned from this chapter about the relationship between benefits and price?

_____

_____

_____

_____

_____

_____

_____

_____

_____

_____

Having gone through the process of deciding on a pricing strategy, what did you find challenging about it and why?

_____

_____

_____

_____

_____

_____

_____

_____

_____

_____

What one thing will you do differently in the future as a result of reading this chapter?

_____

_____

_____

_____

_____

_____

_____

_____

_____

_____

11 THE MARKETING MIX: PLACE

✔ OUTCOMES FROM THIS CHAPTER

- Understand the definition of 'place', the third element of the marketing mix.

- Recognize the relationship between place and promotion.

- Understand the advantages of using distribution channels.

- Know the different distribution channel types and how to make channel strategy decisions.

DEFINING 'PLACE'

Place is the third element of the marketing mix. At its simplest and in probably its original sense, place is where the 'exchange' (of product or service for the price) takes place. Place was originally a market where buyers and sellers could meet to trade. In the modern context, the place part of the marketing mix focuses on how products and services are distributed to customers – which is why this element of the marketing mix is also known as 'distribution'.

We need to distinguish between the physical distribution of products and the channels of distribution:

- **Physical distribution** refers to the *planning, monitoring, and control of the distribution and delivery of manufactured goods*. It is an important part of the process of ensuring that a product is available to customers in the quantities required and when they want to buy.

- **Channels of distribution** refer to the third parties that make the product or service available for use or consumption by the customer.

In considering the marketing mix, we must focus on place as channels of distribution. We can imagine a simple **channel of distribution as** follows:

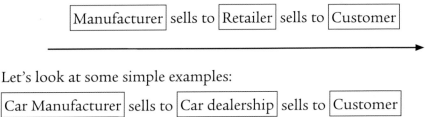

Let's look at some simple examples:

| Car Manufacturer | sells to | Car dealership | sells to | Customer |
| Clothing manufacturer | sells to | Chain store | sells to | Customer |

Services, which are normally sold direct, can also be sold through an intermediary, for example:

| Package holiday | sells to | Travel agent | sells to | Customer |
| Pension company | sells to | Independent financial adviser | sells to | Customer |

The starting point, as with all aspects of the marketing mix, must be the customer. Customers will dictate whether or not we need to use intermediaries or whether we can deal direct.

Products are often distributed through a range of channels (including direct from the originator) simultaneously and the channels can be in competition with one another. The pie chart below shows the breakdown of sales by value of consumer books in the UK for 2010. It shows that chain bookshops and the Internet dominated the distribution of consumer books in the UK in 2010.

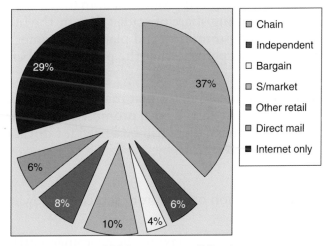

UK consumer books: purchase sources 2010, percentage (%) value
(*Source*: The Publishers Association, 2011)

Clearly, an organization must understand customers' current preferences for where they would like to buy its product. This is known as **channel mapping** and is a key tool in managing the place element of the marketing mix.

Organizations must also monitor changes in the distribution channel sector relevant to their target customers, to assess likely changes that may have an effect on their distribution strategy. For instance, the significant growth in online booksellers such as Amazon has changed the channel map for books in the UK and elsewhere.

 COACH'S TIP

Consider a multi-channel strategy

It is common for products to be present in more than one channel at a time. In our example of the UK consumer book market, while chain bookshops and the Internet dominate this marketplace, supermarkets (at 10-per-cent share) may offer an interesting opportunity for some publishers. Deciding where to position an organization's product across a number of channels is known as a multi-channel strategy.

THE LINK BETWEEN PLACE AND PROMOTION

So far, we have defined the marketing mix as four distinct but related elements of marketing strategy. We have already seen the strong link between product and price (through customers' perceptions of value) and there is a further and increasing relationship between place and promotion. There has been a long tradition of point-of-sale (PoS) promotional material within retail establishments but the increasing share of trade taken by the Internet shows an even stronger link between promotion and place: a customer can view the product online and buy if they perceive that the product has benefits matched to their needs.

Clearly, the nature of the product and, for that matter, the type of customer will dictate whether or not a product can be both promoted and sold via the Internet. For some products and customers, there will be a need for direct interaction with a person. This need is often determined by:

■ the product's complexity

■ whether they need information or help from someone knowledgeable during the purchase process

■ the relative importance of the purchase to the customer, particularly where the purchase is relatively high value.

The relationship between product complexity and relative importance of the purchase is represented in the following model.

Product complexity

The product/purchase matrix

Cell 1 represents a complex and relatively important purchase and is likely to require the involvement of a knowledgeable person through direct interaction. For instance, buying a car is a reasonably complex purchase and of relatively high importance because of the cost and it is generally done at a dealership.

Cell 2 represents a relatively uncomplicated product but one of relatively high importance. Again, there is likely to be a need for some personal involvement but the purchase may be accomplished remotely (e.g. by telephone or email). An example is buying a long-haul holiday.

Cell 3 represents a relatively complex but unimportant purchase. It may be executed via the Internet or use personal interaction. For instance, Dell Computers trade virtually exclusively through the Internet, whereas Apple also trades on the Internet but, in addition, now has a network of Apple retail stores in high-traffic retail locations.

Cell 4 represents a relatively uncomplicated product and a relatively unimportant purchase that is likely to require no personal involvement. An example is buying a train ticket or concert ticket online.

WHY USE INTERMEDIARIES?

If a manufacturer uses a retailer, the retailer must add a cost to the manufacturer's price or take a proportion of the manufacturer's final selling price. For this to make business sense, the retailer must add value to the marketing process. Retailers, or intermediaries in general, add value in a number of ways:

- Dealing with a small number of retailers is more economic for the manufacturer than dealing directly with a large number of end customers.

- For some types of product, the producer would find it very difficult to sell all his output without the support of an intermediary, e.g. farmers selling produce to supermarkets.

- Retailers will take much larger volumes of products than end customers and this offers cost savings to the manufacturer in terms of physical delivery, etc.

- Retailers locate their business operations to meet customers' buying behaviour, e.g. out-of-town shopping centres.

- For some goods, the reputation of the retailer (e.g. Harrods) can enhance their perceived value.

 COACH'S TIP

Focus on the aim of your channel

A channel of distribution can be seen as an array of exchange relationships focused on the ultimate goal of meeting end customers' needs. Building an effective distribution channel requires teamwork between the members of the channel, shared goals and shared investment and return on effort.

CHANNEL TYPES

There are two broad types of channel: intermediaries and direct. Intermediaries are independent organizations that carry out a number of activities associated with adding value to the marketing process. Direct channels are organizations that trade directly with customers.

Intermediaries

There are two main groups of intermediaries: retailers and wholesalers.

Retailers include such organizations as:

- supermarkets (e.g. Tesco, Sainsbury's)
- department stores (e.g. House of Fraser, John Lewis Partnership)
- high-street chains (e.g. Topshop, Next)
- convenience store groups (e.g. Martin McColl, Spar)
- independent retailers, including speciality stores

- franchises – strictly this is not just a channel but a business format model. The franchiser engages with a number of franchisees providing them with a business format (brand, product sourcing, training, publicity, etc.) to extend the franchiser's business coverage and to provide the franchisee with a proven business model. Famous franchise operations include McDonalds, IKEA and Subway.

Wholesalers primarily sell goods and services to those buying for resale and/or business use. They include:

- wholesale merchants – sell primarily to retailers and can be general (i.e. sell a range of products, e.g. Booker Wholesale) or specialist (e.g. fish wholesalers such as M&J Seafood, part of the Brakes Group)

- cash and carry wholesalers – sell from fixed premises and do not normally deliver; buyers come to them for their requirements (e.g. Selco Builders' Warehouse)

- industrial distributors – sell to manufacturers rather than retailers and can carry a range of stock to meet customers' needs (e.g. Nationwide Fuels who supply a range of industrial lubricants to industry in the UK)

- producers' co-operatives – prevalent in the agricultural market, members assemble groups of products to be sold to customers and share the profits.

Direct channels

These are organizations that often choose to trade directly with customers because of cost issues and also because of the potential for building customer relations. Direct channels can be broadly divided into two groups: traditional channels and new media.

Traditional channels are 'traditional' in the sense that these channels have been used for some time. Some of the best-known examples are:

- direct mail – involves posting promotional material direct to the potential customers' home or office and encouraging customers to buy direct (e.g. *Readers' Digest*)

- catalogue-based home shopping – a variant of direct mail, where a catalogue is forwarded to the customer and they are encouraged to purchase products represented in the catalogue (e.g. Littlewoods catalogue)

- inserts – placing promotional material in selected magazines (such as the *Sunday Times* magazine) with instructions for buying direct

- telemarketing – uses the telephone to sell directly to customers, both in consumer and B2B markets

- direct selling – including door-to-door selling and party plan (e.g. Party Plan UK) in consumer markets

- personal selling – this can include own salaried staff and/or sales agents. (Sales forces are common in B2B markets where there is a strong benefit from personal relationships between the salesperson and the buyer.)

- TV shopping – more accurately known as direct-response television marketing (DRTV), DRTV is common in the US and has now become more widespread in other markets such as the UK following the proliferation of satellite and free-to-air channels. DRTV involves the direct promotion of a product to the audience and typically a freephone number for them to make their purchase.

New media have opened up a wide range of new channels for marketers. While of major importance in promotion, the explosion of digital-based technology also offers additional channels of distribution:

- websites – widely used by all sorts of organizations and individuals and often described as 'online shop windows'. Clearly, with the addition of e-commerce (the transactional element), organizations can trade directly with their customers, opening a new channel. Often organizations will have traditional retail channels and in addition, trade direct from their websites

- specialist sites –e.g. eBay has a Seller Development team committed to helping sellers grow their business within the eBay channel

- e-direct mail – used in the same way as traditional direct mail but using email to communicate a particular message or to direct the recipient to a website

- mobile phone marketing – the growth in ownership of smartphones and 3G/4G networks and associated software means that customers can purchase through their mobile phone

- podcasts and vodcasts – are audio and video (respectively) files that can be downloaded to a mobile device. Marketers are experimenting with different approaches to use these technologies as effective channels.

MAKING CHANNEL STRATEGY DECISIONS

The starting point for making distribution channel decisions must always be the customer. Where must our product be placed to be available to customers where they choose to buy? When deciding on which channel to use, we must assess the added value that a channel can provide. We can summarize our distribution channel strategy decisions under three headings in the following checklist:

1. **Current target customer buying behaviour** – we must understand the current behaviour of our target customers and this means:

    i.   understanding where they prefer to buy our products

    ii. mapping channel coverage of our target customers (for each target segment)

iii. monitoring the business environment for potential new entrants (channel level) and/or potential substitute forms of distribution (especially driven by technology).

2. **Competitors' channel behaviour** – we must monitor our competitors' behaviour and this means:

    i. knowing where they place their products in the distribution channels

    ii. tracking changes and/or additions to their channels.

3. **Channel characteristics** – we must have an objective view of the strengths and weaknesses of the channels available to us. This means:

    i. defining the cost benefits of channels in terms of order size, physical distribution economies, etc.

    ii. assessing the added value offered by channels (e.g. product enhancement from being available in a particular channel)

    iii. calculating the cost of using various channels.

COACHING SESSION 37

Your channel strategy decisions

You can now use the channel strategy decisions checklist above to set out your own channel strategy.

Under the headings below, set out for each of your target segments what your distribution channel strategy must contain to meet your objectives.

Target segment 1

Current target customer buying behaviour

_____

_____

_____

Competitors' channel behaviour

_____

_____

_____

Channel characteristics

_____

_____

_____

Target segment 2

Current target customer buying behaviour

_____

_____

_____

Competitors' channel behaviour

_____

_____

_____

Channel characteristics

_____

_____

_____

Target segment 3

Current target customer buying behaviour

_____

_____

_____

Competitors' channel behaviour

_____

_____

_____

Channel characteristics

_____

_____

_____

Target segment 4

Current target customer buying behaviour

_____

_____

_____

Competitors' channel behaviour

_____

_____

_____

Channel characteristics

_____

_____

_____

Once you have completed this list, you can ensure that your decisions are translated into an action checklist (see Chapter 13).

→ NEXT STEPS

In this chapter we have:

- looked at 'place' in the marketing mix and seen that its function is to make products or services available for use or consumption by customers

- distinguished between physical distribution and channels of distribution

- considered the nature of products being available in more than one channel at a time and identified that channels can be in competition with one another (e.g. chain bookshops and the Internet)

- looked at the relationship between place and promotion, particularly with regard to the increasing importance of the Internet in promoting and distributing products and services

- considered the role of intermediaries and looked at how they can add value

- reviewed a range of channel types including intermediaries (such as retailers and wholesalers) and direct (traditional channels and new media)

- set out a distribution channel strategy decisions checklist for you to use in your planning process.

The next chapter will focus on the final element of the marketing mix – promotion. You will find out how to develop a promotional strategy as part of an overall marketing plan. You will learn how the promotional strategy *informs* and *persuades* customers and the steps involved in defining target audiences, setting promotional objectives, creating messages, selecting media, setting budgets and schedules, and evaluation.

 **TAKEAWAYS**

In what ways will you develop your distribution channel strategy to take into account the three factors listed in this chapter – customer buying behaviour, competitors' channel behaviour and channel characteristics?

_____

_____

_____

_____

_____

_____

_____

_____

_____

What have you learned from this chapter about the relationship between place and promotion?

_____

_____

_____

_____

_____

_____

_____

_____

_____

_____

Having gone through the process of deciding on a distribution strategy, what did you find challenging about it and why?

_____

_____

_____

_____

_____

_____

_____

_____

_____

What one thing will you do differently in the future as a result of reading this chapter?

_____

_____

_____

_____

_____

_____

_____

_____

_____

_____

_____

12 | THE MARKETING MIX: PROMOTION

✔ OUTCOMES FROM THIS CHAPTER

- Understand the definition of promotion, the fourth element of the marketing mix.
- Recognize the essential elements of a communication process.
- Know the seven key factors to consider when developing a promotional strategy.

WHAT IS PROMOTION?

Promotion is the final element of the marketing mix. Also called marketing communications, promotion can be seen as the information element of the exchange process we looked at in Chapter 1. Promotion reflects the need for organizations to communicate with their customers and potential customers to support their overall marketing activity. Clearly, if we expend a significant amount of time and effort on understanding customers' needs and developing offerings that carry benefits matched to these needs, then we have to communicate this information to our target audiences.

Organizations have two broad types of audiences:

- current customers
- potential customers.

Promotion can be concerned with three broad issues:

1. **Informing** – providing information about our offerings (creating awareness) or other issues associated with our business (e.g. details of opening times, dates for sales events)

2. **Persuading** – providing persuasive messages (often using information) to persuade customers and potential customers of the benefits inherent in our offering relevant to their perceived needs (i.e. creating a favourable disposition to our offering). In addition, persuasive promotional activity can seek to *differentiate* our offering from that of our competitors, i.e. through more benefits and/or better value than our competitors

3. **Reinforcing** – providing support to customers who have already purchased our offering to remind them of the benefits we offer and to reassure them that they made the right selection decision when choosing our offering.

Promotion can be:

- **impersonal** – through advertisements, public relations or websites

    This can be considered as broadcast media – to a great extent this is one-way communication, in that the receiver does not have a direct line of response. However, research can be used to obtain the reaction of target audiences to our messages.

- **personal** – through direct communication with others

    Whether it is via salespersons or social media (Twitter, etc.), personal promotion allows for two-way communication – it offers an interactive communication medium.

Marketing communications involves developing and delivering co-ordinated messages designed to create a desired effect in a target audience. Ideally, marketing communications should manage the customer relationship over time, from pre-purchase to the purchase stage and through to post-purchase and the brand's ongoing relationship with customers.

THE COMMUNICATION PROCESS

The essential elements of a communication process are:

- **a source** – generally the organization seeking to inform and/or persuade a target audience to adopt a particular view and (ultimately) behaviour

- **a message** – often a combination of words, images and sounds designed so that the target audience can receive the source's intended message and understand it

- **a medium** – a communication channel or channels that will carry the message to the target audience

- **a receiver** – the target audience that is the focus of the communications process.

To maximize the effectiveness of any communication strategy we must start with the target audience (or 'receiver'). We have already seen that customers' motives, values and attitudes (see Chapter 5) influence buyer behaviour and we need to understand our target audience at this level if we are to achieve our promotional objectives. The closer our message is to the target audience's motives, values and attitudes, the more likely it is that we will achieve our promotional objectives.

It is more difficult to obtain our desired result if our audience's attitudes are different from those we would wish them to have. In such a situation, the receiver will adopt one or more of the following behaviours:

- **Selective exposure** – they will avoid messages that are incompatible with their attitudes.

- **Selective perception** – they may distort or misinterpret messages that do not chime with their attitudes.

- **Selective retention** – they will tend to forget more quickly messages that are substantially at odds with their attitudes.

In addition, we need to understand which media 'reach' our target audience: what newspapers/magazines they read, which TV channels and programmes they watch, and so on. Marketing research (see Chapter 5) can be of significant value in providing information to reduce risk in promotional strategy decision-making.

CASE STUDY: THE KELLOGG'S BREAKFAST CLUB CAMPAIGN

Kellogg's is the world's leading producer of breakfast cereals. Manufactured in 18 countries, its products are sold in more than 180 countries. Kellogg's produces some of the world's most recognizable brands, such as Kellogg's Corn Flakes, Coco Pops and Rice Krispies. For more than 100 years, Kellogg's has been providing consumers with a wide variety of food products.

Research commissioned by Kellogg's showed that as many as 1 in 7 children in the UK do not eat breakfast and that up to 25 per cent eat crisps, chocolate or fast food on the way to school. Kellogg's has been supporting breakfast clubs in schools and local communities for many years, but by 2011 they found that 1 in every 8 (around 3,000) breakfast clubs in the UK had closed due to government budget cuts and up to 45 per cent of remaining clubs were at risk of closure.

In response to this, Kellogg's launched their breakfast club campaign, but they needed to make clear that this was not a marketing effort to promote Kellogg's brands but a part of the company's long-standing corporate responsibility programme. Corporate responsibility involves understanding the impact that a business has on the wider community and working to make that impact positive.

The communication plan

The Kellogg's breakfast club campaign had a number of objectives that depended on promoting the right messages to different audiences. Key aims of the campaign were not only to get messages across about the benefits of breakfast and breakfast clubs, but also to raise funds for the clubs through the sale of Kellogg's products and to make schools aware of the available funding from Kellogg's to support their breakfast clubs.

In order to achieve these objectives, Kellogg's devised a communication plan for internal and external stakeholders. The main internal stakeholders targeted were Kellogg's employees who were encouraged to get involved through information posted on the company Intranet. However, the campaign was primarily designed for the needs of external audiences. These included:

- schools – to alert them to the Kellogg's grants available, inviting them to apply for funding
- the media – to generate excitement and press interest about the campaign and to increase public awareness of the issues involved
- parents – to demonstrate Kellogg's socially responsible stance and tell them how breakfast clubs could support their children
- Members of Parliament (MPs) – asking them to encourage schools in their constituencies to apply for funding
- the public – to attract consumers to buy Kellogg's products in order to generate additional funding for the breakfast club initiative.

The campaign used a mixture of formal and informal communications. Formal communications included, for example, press releases and letters sent to MPs. Informal communication involved face-to-face interactions at breakfast clubs and the briefing of 'mummy bloggers'. The problem with informal communication is that it could result in rumours that can cause messages to be mistrusted or even convey inaccurate information.

Campaign evaluation

Kellogg's carried out an evaluation of its campaign:

- The first six weeks of the campaign generated 73 press articles across a variety of media – including news coverage on ITV's *Daybreak* and news articles in *The Observer* and *The Independent*. All carried positive reaction to the messages and reached a potential audience of 9 million people.
- Over 700 schools applied for the funding and around 500 of these received a grant of up to £450 for their breakfast club.
- Kellogg's employees attended 15 of the breakfast clubs with the local MP to see what a difference the funding made to the children.
- The money raised from the campaign provided a million breakfasts by the end of 2012.

(Source and for full case study:

http://businesscasestudies.co.uk/kelloggs/devising-a-communications-plan/#axzz2ZwuKyo1g)

The Kellogg's case study demonstrates the value of research at the outset of the campaign and shows that a campaign can have multiple promotional objectives. The receivers (the target audiences) for this campaign included internal audiences (employees) and a range of external audiences (including schools, media, parents, MPs and the general public). Kellogg's used a range of media (both formal and informal) to carry their message to their target audiences. Finally, as with all good promotional campaigns, Kellogg's initiated evaluation studies to gauge the effect of the campaign and to provide information for similar campaigns in the future.

MAKING PROMOTIONAL STRATEGY DECISIONS

The following seven key decision areas are involved in developing a promotional strategy.

1 Defining the target audience

The strategic process of defining which market segments our organization will target – the 'targeting' exercise – will have enabled us to define and profile the target customers, in terms of both their perceived needs and also their exposure to media (see Chapter 8). The organization may have multiple target segments, each of which is likely to have different characteristics in terms of customer perceived needs and customer profile.

2 Setting promotional objectives

The ultimate objective is likely to be a purchase, so you will need to draft promotional objectives in terms of 'moving' the target audience towards this ultimate aim. A number of writers have suggested that customers move through a series of attitudinal stages:

- starting with **unawareness**
- moving to **awareness**
- developing an **understanding** of the benefits in the offering
- becoming **convinced** that the offering meets their needs
- taking **action** – making the purchase.

It is likely that each of your target segments will give rise to different promotional objectives covering the tasks of informing, persuading and reinforcing described above. For instance, if the target audience is unaware of your organization's offering, the promotional objective is likely to be creating awareness. The case study of XYZ Construction Ltd that we considered in Chapter 3 showed two of their objectives to be focused on (and measured by) awareness and disposition movement:

Objective	Measured by
To establish XYZ as a 'serious' competitor in the new region	Sector market research: • to achieve 60% favourable disposition from decision-makers in the region • to obtain bid opportunities on 50% of 'of interest' projects in the region
To establish strategic relationships with key personnel aligned to the regional market	Sector market research: • 50% awareness and 25% favourable disposition of decision-makers in the region Client relationship management: • engagement with decision-makers in top 20% of client businesses in the region

3 Creating the message/s

The starting point for creating a message is an understanding of the task in hand – knowing our promotional objectives. The message can be informative, persuasive or reinforcing, sometimes all together. A simple, informative message may be something like, 'XYZ Construction has opened an office in your area.'

Persuasive messages form a large part of the media messages we all see and hear every day. In the print media, on the TV and radio, on the Internet and on our smartphones, we receive persuasive messages that have been developed by matching benefits to customers' perceived needs. Often, marketers will seek to focus on the most important needs in the hierarchy of needs (discussed in Chapter 5) as the basis for their messages. The more we know about our target audience, the more effective our messages will be – so marketing research at the pre-campaign stage offers a valuable resource in this context.

A structured approach to message design is based on the acronym AIDA:

- Attention – the first part of the promotional message must capture the attention of the audience by stating something that they can agree with, by defining a problem they may have or a need that is not currently met.

- Interest – the next part must focus on the benefits available from our offering, relevant to these needs.

- Desire – this step seeks to give an imperative to the audience to move to the next step, action.

- Action – the final step can be as simple and low risk for the receiver as 'Contact us for a brochure' or 'Visit our website.' Alternatively, the call to action could be more direct, for example, 'Make a purchase now!' The action we stipulate will depend on our promotional objectives and on the nature of the target audience.

Part of the persuasive message may well be associated with differentiating our offering from that of our competitors. This is likely to involve making comparisons with the benefits offered by the competition and/or the value delivered by them and seeking to establish that our offering is superior.

Messages designed to reinforce customer behaviour tend to be strongly linked to the original persuasive themes to provide a basis for combating post-purchase anxiety.

Message design can also be influenced by the nature of the medium. For instance, an advertisement in a magazine would be able to carry a more detailed message than a TV advertisement because it could be reread, but a TV advert would be able to use a range of techniques including moving images and sounds (music and dialogue), which would have more impact.

4 Selecting the media

Media carry the message/s to the target audiences. There are many media available:

- **Print** – includes national and regional newspapers, the free press, special interest magazines (e.g. music, gardening), age-group targeted magazines (e.g. *Saga Magazine*) and lifestyle magazines (e.g. *Tatler*)

- **TV** – terrestrial, cable and satellite, carries sophisticated multimedia promotional messages

- **Cinema** – can run longer versions of TV adverts and can be targeted at audiences based on the nature of the film being run

- **Commercial radio** – audio advertisements which, like cinema, can be targeted at particular groups based on the content of the programmes being run

- **Personal selling** – a very effective promotional medium where trained and experienced salespeople interact with the customer; often a key part of B2B promotion and high-cost domestic durables (e.g. cars)

- **Direct marketing** – postal, leaflet drop, telephone (including auto dialling)

- **Outdoor poster** – includes large fixed billboards, bus stop, motorway, airport, underground, mobile (vehicle based), inflatables including airborne 'blimps'

- **Public relations** – the discipline that looks after reputation, with the aim of earning understanding and support and influencing opinion and behaviour

 COACH'S TIP

Use PR messages

An important aspect of promotion, PR is the planned and sustained effort to establish and maintain goodwill and mutual understanding between an organization and its public. Key to its success is the ability of the PR practitioner to place press releases in appropriate media.

- **Sponsorship** – cash or in-kind support of anything from small regional events to major international events such as the Olympics and the football World Cup

- **Online** – from websites to sponsored links on search engines to specially designed adverts running on host sites, including social networking sites such as Twitter and Facebook

- **Mobile** – the growth in ownership of smartphones and 3G/4G networks has given advertisers a new medium to deliver promotional messages to peoples' phones based on platforms including mobile browsers, apps (software applications) and SMS (short message service).

Selecting media is very much about the nature of the target audience and the task/s (the promotional objectives) to be accomplished. We must consider the following:

1. Which media best 'reach' the target audience

   By this we mean the number of people who will be exposed to the message carried by the medium. Clearly, the more of our target audience covered by the medium the better.

2. The nature of the task or tasks to be accomplished

   If we wish to make an audience aware of a new car launch, broadcast media may offer the best approach. Once potential customers become interested in the new car, they will require more detailed information and different media are better suited to this, such as brochures, websites, product testing in car magazines and blogs.

3. The relative cost of reaching an audience

   Different media have different costs and reach, and we should seek to create a reasonable comparison by dividing the cost of an advertisement in a particular medium by the reach (or coverage) of that medium – often expressed as a cost per 1,000 audience. This enables us to make like-for-like comparisons of media and helps us select the most cost-effective medium/media to carry our message/s to our target audience/s.

4. What the medium can 'do' for the message

   Some media can enhance the message – for example, exclusive magazines can add value to our brand through its association with the title. On the other hand, some media can detract from the message – for example, if a religious organization's message were to appear on a gambling website page.

5 Creating the promotional programme

The promotional programme has two components: the **mix** of media to be used and the **schedule** of activities over the time of the campaign. The following table shows an example of a simple programme.

Medium	Activity	Month 1	Month 2	Month 3	Month 4
TV	4 × 60 seconds	×		×	
Radio	6 × 20 seconds		×		×
Press	4 × ¼ page	×		×	
Twitter	Weekly feed	×	×	×	×
Public relations	News releases	×		×	

The first column (Medium) lists the media to be used in this campaign. They include broadcast media and a social media 'feed' (allowing personal two-way communication) supported by a public relations (PR) campaign. The next column (Activity) describes the nature of the promotion in each medium. The following columns represent the schedule of promotional activities over a four-month period.

The key is to ensure an *integrated* programme of promotional activity that enables messages to build on earlier work and for themes to be *reinforced* as the campaign progresses. All too often, messages emanate from different parts of the organization, with the result that the customer receives a mixed set of messages – at worst, contradictory – that can seriously reduce the effectiveness of a campaign.

6 Setting the budget

Setting a budget is often a difficult problem. Some organizations base their decision on what is affordable for them. However, this method fails to link what needs to be done (i.e. the promotional objectives) with the resources to do it. Others use a 'percentage of sales' approach and might make, say, 10 per cent of last year's total sales available for this year's promotional budget. Again, this method fails to link the resources to the objectives. Another approach is to match competitors' promotional spend, assuming that this will give the organization parity with them. This approach again fails to focus on the organization's promotional objectives.

Probably the best approach to budget setting is the **objective-and-task** method. This entails assessing what has to be achieved, the tasks involved and the estimated cost of performing these tasks.

7 Evaluating the results

Promotional spend is a business investment and therefore must be measured to assess its effectiveness. Unfortunately, it is very difficult to measure the financial return on promotional spend (e.g. sales and profit) because so many factors influence such measures. Effectiveness therefore must be measured in terms of meeting the promotional objectives. For instance, the objectives of XYZ Construction, discussed above, could be measured through post-campaign marketing research.

COACHING SESSION 38

Your promotional strategy decisions

You can now use the promotional strategy decisions checklist above to set out your own promotional strategy.

Under the headings below, set out for each of your target segments what your promotional strategy must contain to meet your objectives.

Target segment 1

Defining the target audience

_____

_____

_____

Setting promotional objectives

_____

_____

_____

Creating the message/s

_____

_____

_____

Selecting the media

_____

_____

_____

Creating the promotional programme

_____

_____

_____

Setting the budget

_____

_____

_____

Evaluating the results

_____

_____

_____

Target segment 2

Defining the target audience

_____

_____

_____

Setting promotional objectives

_____

_____

_____

Creating the message/s

_____

_____

_____

Selecting the media

_____

_____

_____

Creating the promotional programme

_____

_____

_____

Setting the budget

_____

_____

_____

Evaluating the results

_____

_____

_____

Target segment 3

Defining the target audience

_____

_____

_____

Setting promotional objectives

_____

_____

_____

Creating the message/s

_____

_____

_____

Selecting the media

_____

_____

_____

Creating the promotional programme

_____

_____

_____

Setting the budget

_____

_____

_____

Evaluating the results

_____

_____

_____

Target segment 4

Defining the target audience

_____

_____

_____

Setting promotional objectives

_____

_____

_____

Creating the message/s

_____

_____

_____

Selecting the media

_____

_____

_____

Creating the promotional programme

_____

_____

_____

Setting the budget

_____

_____

_____

Evaluating the results

_____

_____

_____

Once you have completed this list, ensure that your decisions are translated into an action plan (see Chapter 13).

NEXT STEPS

In this chapter we have:

- identified that promotion is about communicating with current and potential customers and is concerned with informing, persuading and reinforcing past behaviour that matches our objectives

- identified that the communications process involves a source, a message, a medium and a receiver

- looked at the detail of promotional strategy decisions and focused on seven key decision areas – defining the target audience, setting promotional objectives, creating the message/s, selecting the media, creating the promotional programme, setting the budget and evaluating the results.

The next chapter will focus on how to 'operationalize' the plan – how to create detailed action plans and how to delegate tasks so that you can achieve the objectives of your marketing plan.

👍 TAKEAWAYS

In what ways will you develop your promotional strategy to take into account the seven key decision areas listed in this chapter?

_____

_____

_____

_____

_____

_____

_____

_____

_____

_____

What have you learned from this chapter about the communications process?

_____

_____

_____

_____

_____

_____

_____

_____

_____

_____

_____

Having gone through the process of deciding on a promotional strategy, what did you find challenging about it and why?

_____

_____

_____

_____

_____

_____

_____

_____

_____

What one thing will you do differently in the future as a result of reading this chapter?

_____

_____

_____

_____

_____

_____

_____

_____

_____

_____

13 IMPLEMENTATION AND ACTION PLANS

✔ OUTCOMES FROM THIS CHAPTER

- Understand strategy implementation in context.
- Grasp the key elements and purpose of action plans.
- Complete your action plans.

IMPLEMENTATION IN CONTEXT

As we have seen, the four key components of marketing planning are analysis, planning, implementation and control. In the marketing planning process model (see Chapter 3), we saw that the analysis and planning stages culminated in action – the implementation stage. The purpose of planning must be to make our actions more effective. Therefore, planning without action is an arid academic exercise and of no real value to the organization. How the plan is implemented is therefore critical.

Key to implementing the strategies we have developed over the previous chapters is the development of action plans, to focus and control the resources available to achieve the objectives of the organization. Action plans are about co-ordinating people and resources within the organization to carry out the tasks dictated by the planning process, so that we increase the probability of achieving the organization's objectives.

There are three key issues contained in the above statement:

1. Co-ordinating people and resources

People get things done. It is people who actually accomplish something. People possess a wide range of skills and abilities but they also come with their own personal objectives, anxieties and prejudices. The most effective planning process is worthless unless we can motivate those involved to fully engage with and adopt and execute the actions necessary to deliver the marketing plan. In addition to the time of those delegated to deliver the plan, implementation often requires other resources, most commonly finance – for primary research, promotional budgets, etc. These resources must be made available in the right volumes and at the right time (as dictated by the planning process) to support the implementation of the plan.

COACH'S TIP

Avoid the pitfalls

Effective marketing planning is, above all, a practical process, so it is important to give those who have to implement it a sense of 'ownership' of the plan. This will help to avoid potential pitfalls.

2. Tasks dictated by the planning process

The purpose of planning must be to make our actions more effective. The planning process provides a logical and rigorous basis for the future commitment of the organization's resources. The investment in marketing planning made by any organization must be supported by senior management – marketing planning cannot be seen as some sort of 'bolt-on' exercise to the 'real' work of the business; if it is, failure is virtually guaranteed.

3. Increase the probability of achieving the organization's objectives

Because the planning process is built on information, this should increase our probability of success because information reduces risk in decision-making. We will make better and more successful decisions with the benefit of information than we would without it.

THE KEY ELEMENTS OF ACTION PLANS

Action plans should be designed to control the delivery of the overall plan. It is critical that these action plans are effective working documents and not simply 'more paperwork'. When embarking on any programme of action, we therefore need to know the answers to some basic questions:

- What are we trying to do?
- When will we start?
- What do we need?
- Can we do it alone, or do we need help (e.g. external consultants)?
- How long will it take?
- How much will it cost?

It is well documented that teams often get caught up in 'doing things', developing a 'tick box' mentality, and forget the *purpose* of the action plan, i.e. the defined end result. Consequently, action plans must be SMART – specific, measurable, attainable, relevant and time-bound.

There are five key elements to action plans:

1. Set operational goals.

2. Establish time limits and deadlines.

3. Communicate and assign tasks and determine action plans for individuals.

4. Develop sales forecasts.

5. Prepare budgets.

1 Set operational goals

Developing our action plans must start from where we are, not where we would like to be. By starting with the targeting exercise, we will have a number of target market segments and for each we will have a defined marketing mix. This work will provide us with a realistic picture of where we are and provide us with our list of high-level activities necessary to achieve our objectives. Setting operational goals is a procedure for the translation of these objectives into discrete and measurable sub-sets of specific goals.

For instance, in the example of XYZ Construction Ltd (see Chapter 3), we took one of the qualitative objectives – 'To establish XYZ as a "serious" competitor in the new region' – and translated it into two quantitative objectives:

■ to achieve 60 per cent favourable disposition from decision-makers in the region (sector market research)

■ to obtain bid opportunities on 50 per cent of 'of interest' projects in the region.

From the first quantitative objective we can create operational goals. Given that this objective is fundamentally a promotional one, the operational goals would be focused on the following sub-sets:

■ Defining the audience

■ Creating the message/s

■ Selecting the media

■ Creating the promotional programme

■ Setting the budget

■ Evaluating the results (already designated for market research).

We would need to ensure that the sum of the sub-sets of activities is both necessary and sufficient to achieve each goal.

COACH'S TIP

Break sub-sets into milestones

To make the process of setting goals easier to control, break each sub-set into a set of milestones – i.e. distinct activities that can be completed as part of the 'journey' to the overall completion of the defined task.

2 Establish time limits and deadlines

Each task requires an organized start, middle and finish. Setting operational goals will create a list of actions and each action can be ascribed a timeline: when it starts, milestones to measure performance during the middle, and when it finishes. Without specific time frames and deadlines, work will definitely expand to fill the time allotted, and some tasks may never be completed.

Some tasks or milestones may seem more daunting to achieve than others. That's when it makes sense to break larger tasks down into smaller, more manageable packages.

Once you've created your action items and set a specific timeline, the next step is to create some type of visual representation of your plan. You might use a flowchart, a Gantt chart, a spreadsheet, or some other type of business tool to accomplish this. Below is an example of a simple Gantt chart:

Task Name	Dec '08	Q1 2009			Q2 2009			Q3 2009	
		Jan '09	Feb '09	Mar '09	Apr '09	May '09	Jun '09	Jul '09	Aug
Planning		▨▨▨▨							
Research			▨▨▨						
Design				▨▨					
Implementation					▨▨▨▨				
Follow up								▨▨	

3 Communicate and assign tasks

Each major activity should have an individual person accountable for its accomplishment. This person does not necessarily have to be the person who does the work, but is the person who will make sure that the work gets done. *Do not* list a function, department or team as the owner; this must be an individual, a single name, because this assures accountability.

There is always the danger of a dislocation between the operational goals of staff (i.e. the things they do as part of their everyday job) and the implementation of the marketing plan. The relevance of the plan, its logical and rigorous basis and its relevance to the future prosperity of the organization must be communicated and reinforced. In fact, there is often a need for an internal communications strategy to manage this change to the culture of the organization effectively.

Progress meetings are important and should be regularly scheduled to review the progress on the action plan. Meetings should be frequent enough to be able to catch potential issues and correct them before they become a problem. These meetings should be brief and focused on problem items and the development of countermeasures to eradicate those problems.

All individuals involved in the implementation should align their personal time management tools (diary, hard-copy day planner, software day planner or smartphone) with the action plan and schedule out their tasks and what they need to accomplish in line with the overall plan.

Once your plan is established and shared with the team, and accomplishments are scheduled, the next step is to take daily action and follow up with the responsible parties to ensure that everyone is doing their part and the plan is 'on track'.

 COACH'S TIP

Don't give up

Occasionally, circumstances or unforeseen events can arise that prevent you from meeting your deadlines, completing tasks and achieving your goal. If this happens, do not be discouraged: revise your plan and continue working to meet targets and move forward. Do not give up on the end objective.

4 Develop sales forecasts

Given that sales (and profitability) are the ultimate measures of the success of our marketing planning effort, it is important that we construct sales forecasts, even if our current position means that we need to achieve a number of other goals before we can realistically expect to make any sales. In the example of XYZ Construction Ltd, we have a situation where an established business is developing a new regional strategic business unit (SBU) and we have seen that the qualitative and quantitative objectives for this planning period are focused broadly on establishing the SBU in its catchment area. However, if we take one of its qualitative objectives, 'To establish XYZ as a serious competitor in the new region', we can focus on one of the quantitative objectives associated with this: to obtain bid opportunities on 50 per cent of 'of interest' projects in the region. The opportunity to bid will ultimately result in sales and from a SWOT analysis we can establish the likely market/segment size, competitive position and from this the likelihood of bidding success. We can then proceed to draft a sales forecast.

In developing such a sales forecast, we would need to consider two key variables:

- value and volume – the monetary order value and the numbers of contracts obtained

- timing – when these contracts are likely to be secured.

Our analysis of the opportunities and threats in the marketplace will help us estimate value and volume and we can make assessments of the timing based on our overall action plan. For instance, if we plan for our awareness/disposition activities to take 8–10 months, we may say that we expect our first contract in month 12. Given that we have to use a high degree of estimation, it is important that sales forecasts are updated as the action plans are rolled out. However, even with this lack of precision, it is still a valuable exercise because it focuses the team's attention on the ultimate outcome of our actions.

 COACH'S TIP

Integrate the functions of sales and marketing

In large organizations, the functions of marketing and sales are not always well integrated. The sales function focuses on today's products, customers and problems, whereas the marketing function also has an additional focus on the future. It is therefore important that what the marketing function is planning, the sales function is doing – that the two functions are part of the same continuum.

5 Prepare budgets

Here we are considering budgeting in the context of marketing planning, rather than as an organization-wide activity. However, our marketing plan must be linked to *all* other functions within the organization and in some situations what we decide to do through the process of marketing planning has an impact on what we do in other functional areas. We may need increased productive capacity (operational function), we may need to train and/or develop staff and perhaps recruit new members of staff (HR function) and all of our actions are likely to require financing (finance function).

A budget is a document that translates our plans into money – money that we will need to spend to get our planned activities done (expenditure) and money that will need to be set aside to cover the costs of getting the work done (finance). It is an estimate of what is needed in monetary terms to execute your plan.

Budgets come from operational plans – in other words, we have to decide what we need to do and then estimate the likely costs associated with those actions.

The costs we need to estimate fall into the following categories:

- **Operational costs** – these are the direct costs of completing the actions/doing the work (e.g. the cost of hiring a venue or of printing a publication). Here you would include materials, equipment, transport and services.

- **Staffing costs** – these are the costs for your core staff – the people involved in managing and delivering the plan, the people doing the work that may cut across departmental cost centres.

- **Capital costs** – these are costs for any large 'investments' necessary to meet the objectives of our plan. These investments – vehicles, computers – will remain organizational assets after the planning programme is completed.

COMPLETING YOUR ACTION PLANS

The next step in developing your marketing plan is to draft your action plans. You should start from the targeting exercise and the selection of your target segments and the development of the marketing mix for each segment (the processes discussed in Chapters 9–12) under the following headings:

- Target segment (Name)
- Product strategy
- Pricing strategy
- Channels strategy
- Promotional strategy.

In each marketing mix element there will be a series of specific tasks required to achieve our objectives. To translate these tasks into action plans, first list all the tasks to be completed. Next, translate these into an action plan format that specifies the task, the necessary action, who is responsible for the effective completion of the task and when the task is to be completed. Below is an example of an action plan format.

Sample action plan format

Task 'name'	Task detail	Objective	Action	By whom	When

We can look at each column in turn.

- **Task 'name'**

  To facilitate easy communication of tasks, it is often useful to give a task a name – perhaps a shortened version of the full description of the task.

- **Task detail**

  To avoid ambiguity, particularly where a team is working on the action plan, it is valuable to set out the detail of the task.

- **Objective**

  This links back to the marketing mix and should ensure that the actions are focused on the desired end result.

- **Action**

  This is a list of the specific actions to be undertaken. It is quite possible that each task will have more than one action. Sometimes actions will need to be completed in a defined order so, in the example of XYZ Construction Ltd, a mailshot may be part of the action necessary to meet the objective defined as 'To achieve 60 per cent favourable disposition from decision-makers in region'. A mailshot would involve sourcing a mailing list, developing a promotional letter, organizing the physical mailing and setting up some follow-up procedures. Some actions can be executed simultaneously (e.g. sourcing a mailing list and developing a promotional letter could be done at the same time) but some must follow in a logical order – for example, we cannot execute the mailing without a mailing list or a promotional letter.

- **By whom**

  This must be a named individual who will be held responsible for the effective and timely execution of the action.

- **When**

  This is an end target for the action, a date when the action will be completed.

COACHING SESSION 39

Preparing your action plans

Now you must prepare your action plans. Start with your target segments and the marketing mix strategies you have developed for each segment. You will have to construct action plans for each target market segment although there may be some linkages which you can co-ordinate once you have drafted your plans.

List all the tasks to be completed.

_____

_____

_____

_____

_____

_____

_____

_____

_____

_____

_____

_____

_____

_____

_____

_____

_____

_____

Now use an action plan format you are comfortable with to define specific actions, individual responsibilities and when the action must be completed.

Launch the action plans with your team and set up monitoring meetings to control progress.

→ NEXT STEPS

In this chapter we have:

- focused on the importance of implementing the plan

- seen how the purpose of action plans must be to make our actions more effective

- looked at the five key elements of action plans – set operational goals, establish time limits and deadlines, communicate and assign tasks and determine action plans for individuals, develop sales forecasts and prepare budgets

- looked at how you would approach preparing your own action plans.

The final chapter will look at how to set up procedures to monitor and control the implementation of the plan and, where necessary, how to put the plan back 'on track' should there be evidence that we will not achieve our objectives. In addition, we will look at the importance of monitoring changes in the market environment and ways of adapting the plan to deal with such changes.

👍 TAKEAWAYS

In what ways will you develop your action plan to take into account the five key elements – set goals, establish deadlines, communicate and assign tasks to individuals, develop sales forecasts and prepare budgets – discussed in this chapter?

_____

_____

_____

_____

_____

_____

_____

_____

_____

What have you learned from this chapter about action planning and implementation?

_____

_____

_____

_____

_____

_____

_____

_____

_____

Having gone through the process of completing and implementing your action plan, what did you find challenging about it and why?

_____

_____

_____

_____

_____

_____

_____

_____

_____

_____

_____

What one thing will you do differently in the future as a result of reading this chapter?

_____

_____

_____

_____

_____

_____

_____

_____

_____

_____

_____

_____

_____

14 MONITORING AND CONTROL

 OUTCOMES FROM THIS CHAPTER

- Understand what monitoring and control mean.
- Recognize that monitoring and control are key components of the marketing planning process.
- Learn ten key points about the marketing planning process as a whole.

WHAT ARE MONITORING AND CONTROL?

As we have seen, the four key components of marketing planning are analysis, planning, implementation and control. Monitoring and control are the procedures needed once we are implementing the plan so that we can keep the plan on track and, if necessary, put it back on track if it seems that we will not achieve our objectives.

In Chapter 13 we discussed the importance of implementation and touched on some of the aspects of monitoring. To control the plan we must monitor its execution, which means that monitoring is inextricably linked to the effective implementation of our plan.

- **Monitoring** is a type of evaluation performed while the plan is being implemented. In essence, we are concerned to ensure that what we say we are going to achieve is actually achieved – it is a comparison of what we had planned to do with what we actually have done.

- **Control** is concerned with taking *corrective action* so that deviation from the plan is minimized and the stated objectives of the plan (and ultimately the organization) are achieved.

COACH'S TIP

Ask three key questions when monitoring

In an effective monitoring system, we are asking three questions:

- Is the plan on track and are we hitting our targets?
- Inside the organization, will any changes affect the successful achievement of our objectives?
- In the marketplace/business environment, will any changes affect the successful achievement of our objectives?

Is the plan on track and are we hitting our targets?

As we have seen, there are five key elements to action plans:

1. Set operational goals.
2. Establish time limits and deadlines.
3. Communicate and assign tasks and determine action plans for individuals.
4. Develop sales forecasts.
5. Prepare budgets.

When we look at the five elements of action plans, the most important element from a monitoring perspective is the fourth one:

'Communicate and assign tasks and determine action plans for individuals.'

Our action plans need to be SMART (specific, measurable, attainable, relevant and time-bound) and this approach also provides a framework for our monitoring system. Encapsulated in this fourth element are all the SMART requirements, offering us a clear focus for control: where we see that we are not achieving what we planned, we can identify exactly what needs to be done and by whom, to recover the situation. To do this, we must ensure that we have up-to-date information on what we have achieved compared with what we had planned to achieve. There are two elements of measurement:

1. **On time** is simply about the action (of an appropriate quality) being completed by the designated time.
2. **To quality** is about checking the quality of the work we have done, to ensure that it is to the standard set in the action plan. If, say, the action is to develop a promotional letter to be used in a mailshot, we have to assess whether the completed text is of appropriate quality for our purposes.

How will changes in the organization affect the plan?

It is inevitable that the organization will change in some way during the implementation of the plan. Staff members may leave or retire, new members may join, there may be changes in the location of the organization, or new products may become available. You could say that these changes can be divided into two groups – those that weaken us (e.g. the loss of a key member of staff may create a problem for us in the short or medium term) and those that strengthen us (e.g. a new member of staff may have skills and experience that were not previously held in our organization and can enhance our skill base). Consequently, we have two approaches for dealing with these changes:

1. For changes that may weaken us, we need to identify them, assess their likelihood of occurring and set out what we can do to minimize their effect. This is often known as risk management and it is all about working out what could go wrong and planning what to do if it does.

2. For changes that may strengthen us, we need to consider how we would integrate them into our current plan. Clearly, having worked through the marketing planning process, we have been able to make some key decisions based on sound evidence, such as which market segments we should target (a key decision in terms of the success of the organization), so anything that strengthens us must be considered in the light of the current plan.

How will changes in the marketplace/business environment affect the plan?

Our market and business environment is always changing, sometimes gradually and sometimes quite dramatically:

- Customers' needs and behaviour (in terms of how they buy, for instance) can evolve or change dramatically.

- Competitors can become stronger or weaker and they can change their strategies.

- PEST factors can create threats and opportunities.

By implementing our plan, we may also cause a reaction from our competitors (direct competitors, new entrants and substitutes). To paraphrase the nineteenth-century Prussian General Moltke, 'No plan of operations extends with any certainty beyond the first contact with the main hostile force.' Consequently, we need to ensure that we *monitor* our marketplace/business environment to scan for changes that could affect the success of our plan. Having already conducted a wide-ranging and thorough market audit, we will have in place the sources and methods to continue to monitor our marketplace/business environment.

Again, the issue of *control* becomes important here. It is pointless to monitor our marketplace/business environment unless we are prepared to act if we see anything that may affect the successful implementation of our plan. All too often, managers finalize their planning document and action plans and then see the plan as sacrosanct (i.e. not to be touched). This is a major mistake – our plan must respond to the real world, not the world we would like to exist. The tasks of analysis and planning are there simply to increase the probability that we will achieve our objectives. To do this, our plan must be based on what is currently happening in our marketplace/business environment and, if this changes, we must assess our plan in the light of these changes.

Evaluation

We must also consider evaluation as an essential part of the marketing planning process. Evaluation studies the outcome of the planning process with the aim of informing the design of future planning processes. This takes us to the relationship between monitoring an existing plan and commencing a new planning round.

- Most organizations that embrace marketing planning work to a three-year rolling planning cycle. Each plan is designed to cover a three-year period and, towards the end of that period, the planning process starts all over again, from setting marketing objectives right through to drafting action plans.

- However, as we have seen, if changes occur (either within the organization or within its marketplace/business environment) that are of sufficient magnitude to affect the achievement of our objectives, we must 'revisit' the plan and, where necessary, take action to respond to these changes so that we can successfully complete the plan. This means that, should a major change occur, even within the first month of the implementation stage, we still need to revisit the plan.

 COACH'S TIP

Respond to changes

When you monitor the plan by asking the questions outlined above, the key question is whether any changes, within or outside the organization, will affect the achievement of the objectives. If so, you will have to revisit the plan.

MONITORING AND CONTROL IN THE MARKETING PLANNING PROCESS

The marketing planning process is a chain of interconnected parts, all linked together and all of equal importance in delivering our corporate objectives. It is easy for management to be lulled into a false sense of security – we have committed a significant amount of effort to the analysis and planning stages and now we have set up our action plans so there's nothing more to do than to let the implementation take its course and we shall meet our objectives. This is a major mistake. To ensure a successful outcome, we must 'manage' the implementation stage, and monitoring and control are the processes by which we achieve this management.

Monitoring must be linked to action. If we are not 'on track', we must act to address this. Too often, managers take a laissez-faire attitude, believing that the plan will correct itself. It cannot and therefore will not. That is why organizations need managers – to manage, to respond to changes and to act accordingly.

 COACH'S TIP

Warning

Do not allow all your hard and conscientious work to fail to deliver the defined outcomes of your planning process simply because the plan was not properly monitored and controlled.

COACHING SESSION 40

The key stages in your monitoring system

Starting with your action plans, set out the key stages in your monitoring system, ensuring that you cover the following questions.

Is the plan on track? Are we hitting our targets?

_____

_____

_____

_____

_____

Are there any changes within the organization that will affect the successful achievement of our objectives?

_____

_____

_____

_____

Are there any changes within our marketplace/business environment that will affect the successful achievement of our objectives?

_____

_____

_____

_____

Be ready and committed to take action where necessary.

HOW TO SUCCEED WITH MARKETING PLANNING

You should now be at the beginning of your marketing planning activity. The process described in this workbook is based on best practice and is associated with improved business performance. Marketing should be seen as an approach to running an organization, not simply a function within the organization. That means that everyone within the organization must understand and believe in the importance of matching the organization to customers' needs and not attempting to fit the customer to the organization.

Leadership is inextricably linked to effective marketing planning. The CEO, senior managers, middle managers and team leaders must all understand and value marketing. If senior staff think marketing is simply a fancy name for advertising or selling, then you can guarantee that the marketing plan will not deliver any benefits to the organization. All levels of management must be 'on message' – they must understand and believe in the benefits of marketing for the organization's survival and prosperity.

Often, managers see the marketing planning process as a daunting task – and one that is additional to their normal workload. In addition, some have even described the process as too rigid for them to adopt. Such feelings are understandable and it is quite acceptable to adapt or customize the marketing planning process to meet the characteristics and current situation of you and your organization. However, it will be essential to adopt the key themes if you are to obtain any real benefit from the process.

It is the customers who pay our salaries, not our boss or the MD or the business: anyone who has been made redundant when their employer went into liquidation will know this. To avoid business failure, we must stress the need to satisfy customers if we are to survive and prosper.

Marketing planning must not stifle creative thinking and there is no reason why it should. The process provides a framework within which we can deal with complex multifaceted problems, is founded on the value of information to reduce risk and allows for change to be addressed. A new idea or solution to a customers' need can be accommodated within the process. In fact, the very process of gauging and measuring those needs can lead to the development of new approaches to meeting those needs.

COACH'S TIP

Use marketing planning to see opportunities

Fundamentally, marketing planning makes the organization outward looking and raises awareness of how best to match the strengths of the organization to opportunities in the marketplace.

HOW LONG DOES THE PROCESS TAKE?

The time it takes to complete the full marketing planning process depends on a number of factors, including:

- the size and complexity of the organization
- the number and nature of staff available to work on the process
- the quality and availability of in-house data
- whether the organization has up-to-date information on customers' attitudes and perceptions.

However, given a medium-sized organization with good internal data systems, one could expect the process to take seven to eight months. This is demonstrated in the following model of the duration of a typical marketing planning process. You will notice that the task with the longest duration is primary research with customers.

Typical marketing planning process duration

Stage	Month 1	Month 2	Month 3	Month 4	Month 5	Month 6	Month 7
Set marketing objectives	■						
Business audit	■						
Market audit:							
– Customer (secondary)		■					
– Customer (primary)		■					
– Competitors			■				
– PEST				■			
SWOT				■			
Targeting exercise					■		
Four Ps*					■		
Action plans						■	
Monitoring & control format						■	
Launch							■

*NB for each target segment

THE TOP TEN TIPS OF MARKETING PLANNING

1. Make sure your organization is truly marketing oriented – that everyone understands that, if we do not satisfy customers' needs, we cannot expect to survive and prosper.

2. Make everyone in the organization part of the marketing process – make them outward looking and ensure that everyone knows what they must do to meet customer needs, are trained and equipped to do so and are motivated to do it.

3. Understand your customers' needs – now and what they may be in the future. This means obtaining objective, unbiased and robust information that will reduce risk in decision-making. While information in the public domain is very useful, to get a unique insight you need to commission your own research, which only your organization can see.

4. Monitor your competitors, current, potential new entrants and substitutes. Be able to talk fluently about your competitors' strengths and weaknesses, what their strategies are and what direction they are travelling in. Be prepared to take action when you see either an opportunity or a threat.

5. Keep one eye on the PEST environment; scan news items, etc., for any opportunities or threats that there may be in the near future.

6. Make 'Information reduces risk' your mantra. If you don't know, don't guess; find out. But remember, 20 per cent of the information you gather accounts for 80 per cent of the reduction in risk in your decision-making. Be alert to the relative value of Information and don't allow yourself to be submerged by data.

7. Market targeting is strongly linked to organizational performance – matching our strengths to market segments is the foundation of a successful plan. Be disciplined in your selection of target market segments and make sure that your marketing mix (the four Ps) are truly aligned to each target market segment.

8. There are four elements to effective marketing planning – analysis, planning, implementation and monitoring. Keep in mind that the first two elements are simply about making implementation *more* effective. Implementation is the step that delivers improved performance (and monitoring helps to keep the plan on track) and is the only point of the analytical and planning stages.

9. Make monitoring a central part of your management tasks – too many plans fail simply because they have been launched by the management team and then ignored, assuming that the plan can run itself. This is not the case, and plans need ongoing support to ensure that they stay on track. Also, remember to monitor the marketplace and general environment for changes that can have a serious impact on the plan in its current format.

10. The marketing planning process is based on best practice and has been shown to deliver improved performance. However, it is critical that we do not become a slave to the process – it is simply a tool for our use. It is better to have a plan 97 per cent complete and being implemented than waiting until it is 100 per cent perfect.

→ NEXT STEPS

In this chapter we have:

- looked at what monitoring and control mean
- considered monitoring and control as key components of the marketing planning process
- looked at a summary of how to succeed with marketing planning
- learned ten key points about the marketing planning process as a whole.

We hope you have found this workbook interesting and useful and now feel equipped to set out on your own marketing planning process. You can now go back to Coaching session 7 and assess how well you believe the workbook has met your personal objectives.

I wish you every success in the future. Good luck!

👍 TAKEAWAYS

In what ways will you develop your monitoring and control process to take into account the three key questions discussed in this chapter?

_____

_____

_____

_____

_____

_____

_____

_____

_____

_____

_____

_____

What have you learned from this chapter about monitoring and control?

_____

_____

_____

_____

_____

_____

_____

_____

_____

_____

_____

_____

Having gone through the process of developing your monitoring system, what did you find challenging about it and why?

_____

_____

_____

_____

_____

_____

_____

_____

_____

_____

What one thing will you do differently in the future as a result of reading this chapter?

_____

_____

_____

_____

_____

_____

_____

_____

_____

_____

APPENDICES

APPENDIX 1

Notes to Coaching session 2

Rank the following factors in terms of your view of how important they are in determining whether or not a business is marketing oriented.

Being the cheapest – while it is obviously important to keep costs and therefore prices low, having the cheapest product is not necessarily related to a marketing orientation. Firstly, we must be sure that our product carries benefits matched to the customers' needs. If we fail to do that, having the lowest price will not help in the medium term because customers will seek alternative products that provide the best value – i.e. the most benefits at the lowest price.

Understanding customers' perceived needs – this is fundamental to being marketing oriented. Understanding customers' perceived needs means we are in a much stronger position to develop products that carry benefits *matched* to these needs.

Having the highest quality product – similar to the lowest price, product quality is obviously important. However, we must have the *right* level of quality matched to the customers' perceived needs. A product with more benefits than the customer requires may be rejected because it is also too expensive – for example, trying to sell a Rolls Royce when the customer wants a Mini.

Having the largest advertising budget – having suitable resources to inform and persuade customers that your product has benefits matched to their needs is important. However, a large advertising budget will not compensate for a product that is poorly matched to the customers' perceived needs.

Having a world-famous celebrity endorse one's product – we are all familiar with celebrities and sports stars being used to endorse products as part of an advertising campaign. Such endorsements can embellish the brand and the association with a celebrity can transmit positive messages that would be difficult to replicate in other forms of communication. However, we must return to the point that, just like heavy advertising spend, celebrity endorsements will not compensate for a product that is poorly matched to the customers' perceived needs.

Having an ongoing investment in marketing research – understanding customer needs is critical for all organizations. In addition, we know that attitudes and perceptions change over time, so an ongoing research activity is fundamental. In essence, information reduces risk in decision-making and managers who have access to the right information make the best and most successful decisions.

Having an ongoing focus on competitors and the general business environment – in the same way that marketing research is important to the success of an organization, monitoring both the actions and strategies of one's competitors and the general business environment is very important for any organization to maximize their probability of success.

APPENDIX 2

Notes to Coaching session 21

Using data on turnover and contribution to analyse strengths and weaknesses

Strengths	
Overall	• While total contribution is down 15%, 2012 on 2010, this is significantly better than turnover performance in the same period (see weaknesses). • Overall contribution rose from 9.9% in 2010 to stand at 14.6% in 2011 and remain at that level (14.3%) for 2012, giving an average for the period of 12.5%.
Product	• In the most recent year (2012) Products 3 and 5 accounted for 70% of total turnover. • Product 5 showed modest growth (5%), 2012 on 2010. • Overall contribution to turnover for the period (2010–12) was 12.5%; the best performer was Product 1 at 17.7%. • Product 5, the second-largest element of turnover in 2012, delivered the second-best contribution figures (14.4%) in the same year.
Segment	• Segment B accounts for 83% of total turnover for the most recent year and showed the lowest fall (−28%), 2012 on 2010. • Segment C provides the best contribution to turnover % at 19% over the period and the best single year: 24.7% in 2010.
Weaknesses	
Overall	• Total turnover is down 41%, 2012 on 2010. • The average contribution for the period was 12.5%, however, there were significant variations from product to product (e.g. Product 1 in years 2011 and 2012) and for the same product from year to year (e.g. Product 4).
Product	• Product 3, the largest single element of turnover in 2010, fell 48%, 2012 on 2010. • Products 2 and 4 fell significantly 2012 on 2010 (88.5% and 62.4% respectively). • Contribution to turnover has been very variable for all products during the period.
Segment	• All segments showed a fall in turnover over the period, the worst being Segment D (−84%), Segment C (−74%) and Segment A (−65%). • Segment A showed the biggest fall in contribution to turnover for the period, down 127%.

APPENDIX 3

Answers to Coaching session 29

Comparing competitor data: using the information in the table to answer questions

1. In the most recent year, which business was the market leader?

   Competitor D

2. In the most recent year, which business had the best operating profit to turnover performance?

   Competitor B

3. In the most recent year, which business had the best productivity (i.e. turnover to number of employees)?

   Client

4. In the most recent year, which business had the worst return on capital employed?

   Competitor C

5. Which business had the biggest fall in turnover most current year on previous year?

   Competitor C

APPENDIX 4

Notes to Coaching session 31

Useful websites for the PEST analysis:

Political

Start by looking at legislation websites.

This lists all current UK acts:

www.legislation.gov.uk/

In addition, the following site provides an alphabetical list of the bills (to be considered for enactment):

http://services.parliament.uk/bills/

As a member of the European Union, the UK is also subject to the laws of the EU:

http://ec.europa.eu/eu_law/introduction/what_regulation_en.htm

Economic

There are a number of sources of information regarding the economy. A good place to start is the Government's Department for Business, Innovation & Skills:

www.gov.uk/government/organisations/department-for-business-innovation-skills

In addition, there are a number of professional and trade bodies that also provide useful information, for example, CBI and Institute of Directors:

www.cbi.org.uk/business-issues/economy/

www.iod.com/your-business-topics?category={191EF422-738C-4A0D-94A6-23907B66F905}

The general and specialist press also provides commentary and analysis on the economy, for example the *Financial Times* and *The Economist*:

www.ft.com/world/uk/economy

www.economist.com/

In addition, many sectors have specialist interest groups or trade bodies. The Society of Motor Manufacturers and Traders (SMMT) exists to support and promote the interests of the UK automotive industry at home and abroad. As part of its service, SMMT provides a review of the economy as it affects its members:

www.smmt.co.uk/industry-topics/economy/#

There are also commercial providers who charge a fee for their services, e.g.:

www.experian.co.uk/economics/about-us.html

Societal

The Office for National Statistics (ONS) provides a range of sources, including population trends:

www.ons.gov.uk/ons/index.html?vlnk=6303

www.ons.gov.uk/ons/rel/population-trends-rd/population-trends/no--145--autumn-2011/index.html

In addition, ONS publishes research concerning social trends:

www.ons.gov.uk/ons/rel/social-trends-rd/social-trends/social-trends-41/index.html

The Census (conducted once a decade) provides an important picture of the UK, including a demographic view:

www.ons.gov.uk/ons/guide-method/census/2011/index.html

Technological

The Chartered Institute of Building Services Engineers represents the interests of those working in the building services industry and this includes providing technical support and monitoring technological developments:

http://cibse.org/

APPENDIX 5

Your action plan

Goal	Task

Goal	Task

QUICK HELP

Here are the key ideas from the book, to use as an aide-memoire.

1 WHAT IS MARKETING?

There are differences between the widely used traditional definition of marketing (from the CIM) and their more recent definition for the twenty-first century.

Focusing on customers' needs is fundamental to achieving an organization's businesses objectives.

The key activities associated with marketing in your own organization are identifying customer needs, market segmentation and the marketing mix (the four Ps).

The key behaviours that characterize a marketing-oriented organization are market sensing, quality focus, internal 'marketing', adaptive response and (good) external relationships.

2 THE BENEFITS AND PITFALLS OF MARKETING PLANNING

Marketing planning is more about management behaviour than simply managers saying that they engage with marketing planning.

Formal marketing planning is associated with better organizational performance.

Marketing planning is a practical process with a clear relationship between strategy and tactics.

If a marketing planning exercise does not deliver improved performance, this is in most cases because of one or more well-documented pitfalls.

3 THE MARKETING PLANNING PROCESS

The seven key stages of the marketing planning process are: set objectives, business audit, market audit, the 'targeting' exercise, defining the marketing strategy, implementation and monitoring.

There are two broad aspects to marketing planning: thinking and doing.

Corporate objectives concern the purpose and nature of the organization.

Marketing objectives are concerned with achieving defined outcomes specific to marketing (i.e. customers and markets).

There are differences and links between corporate and marketing objectives.

It is useful to start from a qualitative articulation of objectives and then translate these into quantitative, measurable targets upon which a strategy can be based and measured.

4 THE BUSINESS AUDIT

The purpose of the business audit is to review the strengths and weaknesses of the organization and to match organizational capabilities with market opportunities.

A SWOT analysis will identify the strengths and weaknesses within your organization and the opportunities and threats within your business environment.

The business audit takes a holistic view of the organization to assess its strengths and weaknesses from the point of view of the marketplace.

The market audit is a comprehensive, systematic, periodic evaluation of an organization's marketing capabilities.

5 THE MARKET AUDIT: CUSTOMERS

The market audit is the assessment of the opportunities and threats that exist in the business environment in which we operate.

The first stage of the market audit is to look at customers and potential customers – in particular the opportunities and threats they present.

Customers' perceived needs for products and services are affected by their motives, values and attitudes.

Important aspects of the market audit are effective market segmentation, customer behaviour and the stages involved in making a purchase.

We can obtain information on customers from a variety of sources to help us in the marketing planning process.

6 THE MARKET AUDIT: COMPETITORS

The four main areas of competitor analysis are performance, objectives, strategies, and strengths and weaknesses.

We can improve our chances of winning if we understand our opponent's strengths and weaknesses – the main reason for conducting competitor analysis as part of a market audit.

Competitors may be categorized as direct competitors (those currently targeting the same customer segments as you), new entrants (those not currently targeting your customer segments but likely to in the future) and substitute offerings (new or different ways to satisfy the same needs of our target customer segments as our offerings).

7 THE MARKET AUDIT: THE MARKETPLACE

The third and final part of the market audit is the PEST analysis, which looks at the political, economic, societal and technological 'environment'.

Sources of information on PEST factors include official, government and commercial sources.

We can draw together all the stages of our audit to produce a consolidated market audit.

Information gathering and analysis can be part of the marketing information system within the organization and is a useful way to capture, analyse and disseminate such information in the future.

8 SWOT ANALYSIS AND STRATEGIC POSITIONING

A consolidated SWOT analysis is based on the strengths and weaknesses identified in the business audit along with the opportunities and threats identified in the market audit.

A strategic positioning or targeting exercise will help the organization decide which segments to focus on.

9 THE MARKETING MIX: PRODUCT

The marketing mix (the four Ps) involves deciding what to produce, how much to charge, where the customer will buy the product and how to inform and persuade the customer to buy the product.

The strategic positioning exercise is related to the development of the marketing mix or strategy.

We need a separate marketing mix for each of our target segments.

The product strategy must carry benefits that satisfy customers' needs, which makes it the fundamental basis of the relationship between the organization and the customer.

Product features are different from benefits, which may be tangible or intangible, and marketing needs to focus on benefits rather than features.

Products have a life cycle and there is a need for new product development within the organization.

10 THE MARKETING MIX: PRICE

Price is inextricably linked to product strategy because customers make judgements about value based on the benefits in the product matched to their needs and the price of the product.

Our pricing strategy needs to meet organizational objectives based on the three forces that affect pricing decisions.

Price is not the same as cost. Price is ultimately controlled by customers' value perceptions; cost is the monetary value of producing and delivering the product, including profit.

11 THE MARKETING MIX: PLACE

The third stage of the marketing mix – place – is where we make decisions that focus on how to make our offering available to customers.

Distribution channels of various types include intermediaries (such as retailers and wholesalers) and direct (traditional channels and new media).

Distribution channel strategy must take into account customer buying behaviour, competitors' channel behaviour and channel characteristics.

We can use various methods to assess the 'added value' an intermediary brings to the marketing mix.

Products may be available in more than one channel at a time and channels can be in competition with one another.

Place is related to promotion, particularly with regard to the increasing importance of the Internet in promoting and distributing products and services.

12 THE MARKETING MIX: PROMOTION

Promotion is about communicating with current and potential customers and is concerned with informing, persuading and reinforcing past behaviour that matches our objectives.

The communications process involves a source, a message, a medium and a receiver.

Promotional strategy is focused on seven key decision areas – defining the target audience, setting promotional objectives, creating the message/s, selecting the media, creating the promotional programme, setting the budget and evaluating the results.

13 IMPLEMENTATION AND ACTION PLANS

To implement the marketing plan, we need to create detailed action plans and delegate tasks so that we can achieve the objectives set out in the plan.

The purpose of action plans must be to make our actions more effective.

The five key elements of action plans are: set operational goals; establish time limits and deadlines; communicate and assign tasks and determine action plans for individuals; develop sales forecasts; and prepare budgets.

14 MONITORING AND CONTROL

Monitoring and control are key components of the marketing planning process.

We need procedures to monitor and control the implementation of the plan and, where necessary, to put the plan back 'on track' should there be evidence that we will not achieve our objectives.

An effective monitoring system checks for changes within the organization that may affect the successful achievement of our objectives.

Monitoring and control also looks at changes in the market environment and ways of adapting the plan to deal with such changes.

INDEX